When All
Doors Close

Desiree A. Pfister

When All Doors Close

Desiree A. Pfister

Publisher

When All Doors Close

Copyright © 2017 by Desiree A. Pfister

All rights reserved. No part of this book may be reproduced, stored in a retrieval system or transmitted in any way by any means—electronic, mechanical, photocopy, recording or otherwise—without the prior permission of the copyright holder, except for brief quotations as provided by USA copyright law.

Printed in the USA

ISBN 978-1-941173-18-3

Published by
Olive Press Messianic and Christian Publisher
www.olivepresspublisher.org
olivepressbooks@gmail.com

Our prayer at Olive Press is that we may help make the Word of Adonai fully known, that it spread rapidly and be glorified everywhere. We hope our books help open people's eyes so they will turn from darkness to Light and from the power of the adversary to God and to trust in ישוע Yeshua (Jesus). (From II Thess. 3:1; Col. 1:25; Acts 26:18,15 NRSV *New Revised Standard Version* and CJB, the *Complete Jewish Bible*)

Cover art and design by Amitabha Naskar.
Interior design by Cheryl Zehr, Olive Press Publisher.
Title page photo © Cheryl Zehr

NOTE: Having a British author and an American publisher, the choice was made to keep some of the British flavor in the grammar and spelling, for example: double "l" in travelling, travelled, travellers, counsellor, counselling, etc., and words like "whilst" vs "while," "queue" vs "line," "centre" vs "center," "honour" vs "honor," etc. Most of the punctuation; however, [except for the semi-colon before every mid-sentence *however*, for example] is more American than British.

All Scripture is taken from the *New King James Version of the Spirit Filled Life Bible*®. Copyright © 1980-1991 by Thomas Nelson, Inc.

Foreword

The Christian life is often a life of waiting, where faith is tested in a battlefield of discouragement and all doors seem to close. This is not a time to despair but to prepare, for the Holy Spirit is continually at work within us, in the quiet times and in the busy times. If we knew all the wonderful things God had in store for us and we knew they were just around the next corner, how would we spend our time waiting? Trusting Him to work all things together for our good enables us to enjoy fellowship with Him in the quiet seasons, so that when the door opens, we'll be ready to share with joy, the hope of the Cross and the promise of everlasting life.

Our call is two-fold:

- The Great Commandment – To *love God with all your heart, soul and strength.* [1]
- The Great Commission – To go *into all the world and preach the gospel.* [2]

We are to be His witnesses in Jerusalem and in all Judea and Samaria, and to the ends of the earth. [3] It is true that not everyone can leave their homelands; some of us are meant to stay and serve at home, while others are called to Judea, Samaria and the ends of the earth. For those who stay, the lost, the poor and the downhearted are always close by. The Great Commission can be accomplished whether at home or on an overseas mission.

I had the desire at a young age to fulfill the Great Commission overseas, but all those doors were closed. So, my journey started with a call to serve in my native country first, and then, after more than a twenty year wait, the door was finally opened for me to leave my family and my country and cross the cultural divide to lands I never dreamed of ever visiting. Some of these areas were places that had greatly impacted the development of the early church, like Cappadocia, the home of the first Christians mentioned in the book of Acts, Prague where the seed of Reformation was first planted, and Scotland and Wales, the lands of great revivals. Then, miraculously, I was finally able to fulfill my dream of serving in China. And, not forgetting the most important land of all, I was also sent to Israel, where recent archaeological discoveries have confirmed the arrival of the Israelites in Canaan.

God is still doing extraordinary things through ordinary people. If you are serving the Lord as an overseas missionary, or at home in your own country, each new day presents itself with opportunities to share the Good News. If you feel you could be doing more, reach out beyond your boundaries to wherever the Lord leads. He has a plan for you and He will bring it to pass. If you have been waiting a long time for the Lord to use you, be encouraged. The Lord will open the doors; you only need to take the first step.

Contents

Foreword		6
1	The Preparation	11
2	Rivers of Living Water	29
3	When All Doors Close	43
4	Prague	47
5	Visas and Vestibules	59
6	Land of Beautiful Horses	65
7	God of China	87
8	Land of Dragon	95
9	Teacher, Tell Me About God	107
10	An Appointed Time	115
11	He Calls His Own	121
12	No Monkeys in Heaven	127
13	Tombs and Travel Lessons	133

14	An Angel in Intensive Care	143
15	Questions about Life	147
16	The Culture of Christmas	155
17	Leaving the Land of Dragon	161
18	The Next Step	167
19	Chaos and Cancelled Flights	175
20	The Garden Tomb	179
21	From Bethlehem to Megiddo	189
22	The Welsh Outpouring	197
23	Land of the Long White Cloud	201
24	A Door of Hope	205
25	Into All the World	211
Reference Notes		218

Kwa-Zulu Natal

1
The Preparation

Trust in the Lord, and do good: Dwell in the land, and feed on His faithfulness.

Psalm 37:3

GROWING UP WITH A SWISS father in the multicultural society of South Africa helped me to appreciate the diversity of the values and beliefs of others. Our home was a hive of activity. My four brothers and I kept our mother busy. My father was fluent in four languages, and when he was agitated he would yell at us in all of them.

As a young man, and avid explorer, he ventured into uncharted territories of Portuguese East Africa, (now Mozambique) where he contracted malaria and black-water fever, which left him plagued with migraines. We had to learn to keep the sound levels down a bit, but with five lively children, it required some "quiet management."

My father had a plant nursery at our home where he specialized in cacti and succulents, which he imported and exported all over the world. He would retreat to his plants to escape the hubbub of the household, and when the noise filtered down to the nursery, we would all be summoned to gardening chores. Packing and unpacking prickly pears and other spikey specimens required careful attention, so silence ensued for a while.

My father would tell us stories of his travels and adventures, and his close encounters with dangerous animals, and there, the desire to experience life in other lands was seeded in me. My parents were both exposed to the Gospel in their upbringing, but my father chose to be agnostic. Thank the Lord for testimonies and for those who faithfully share them.

One of my aunts, who has now gone to be with the Lord, received a miracle healing from arthritis whilst seeing Jesus in a vision. He first appeared to her at her bedside one night in hospital, and again in the morning when the doctors came to tell her it was unlikely she would ever walk again. She promptly slipped down from the bed and went after Jesus as she saw Him walk towards the door. She then followed the Lord faithfully for the rest of her life until the day He took her home.

It was enough to convince me Jesus was alive, but my twelve year old mind succumbed to a lie that a person could only be a Christian if you came from a Christian home. The enemy held me in that grip for nearly seven years, until—one day—I decided to ask God myself. And to my surprise, He accepted me. The presence of the Holy Spirit surrounded me, and I immediately flowed with thanksgiving. How easily we can be deceived. Anyone can be part of God's family, whether we are raised in a Christian home or not, we all need to be spiritually reborn. This is a gift of grace that cannot be earned.

For by grace you have been saved through faith, and that not of yourselves; it is the gift of God, not of works, lest anyone should boast. — Ephesians 2:8-9

1 The Preparation

From that day, my name was registered in the Lord's book and my citizenship in heaven secured. Psalm 87 became my "born again Psalm."

> And of Zion it will be said, "This one and that one were born in her; and the Most High Himself shall establish her." The Lord will record, when He registers the peoples: "This one was born there." — Psalm 87:5-6

My enthusiasm in my new faith was faced with much scepticism at home, but I toughened up quickly and stood my ground. I felt an urgency to share the Gospel with my two younger brothers, having no idea then, how crucial it was as their lives were soon cut short. They both died within a twelve-year period as young men, after ongoing battles with chronic illnesses that resulted in severe depression and ended in suicide. God prepared me for their deaths in dreams, and I have since never doubted that the Lord's hand is not too short to reach out and save the lost in their final hour. Knowing I had planted seeds of faith in my brothers was a great comfort to me, and together with the dreams the Lord gave me, left me with a peaceful assurance that they were safe with Him.

> Oh, the depth of the riches both of the wisdom and knowledge of God! How unsearchable are His judgments and His ways past finding out! — Romans 11:33

People often asked if suicides can go to heaven. It's not the act of taking one's life that sends people to hell any more than good works can earn us a place in heaven. Accepting, or rejecting Jesus as our Saviour is what determines our destiny. He alone can forgive sins.

God is on the Throne. He sees the end from the beginning and knows all things even before they happen—not even a sparrow falls to the ground apart from Him (Matthew 10:29).

> *Do not say in your heart, "Who will ascend into heaven?" (that is to bring Christ down from above) or, "Who will descend into the abyss?" (that is to bring Christ up from the dead).*
> — Romans 10:7-8

I've spoken to many people over the years who have dealt with the death of a loved one. Some say it changes their outlook on life and how they spend their time. For others, it increases their interest in eternal values and the world seems less appealing. I turned my attention to studying God's Word and pursued every available course that came my way; from Bible surveys, discipleship and evangelism, Psalms and worship, to a Bachelor of Theology and eventually a Masters in Christian counselling. I studied fervently and argued unswervingly with my father about the Bible, the reality of God, heaven, and hell. My father was unyielding, but the Word of God proved more powerful, and never returns void (Isaiah 55:11). My father eventually repented and accepted Jesus as his Saviour two weeks before he passed away at the age of ninety-one. His deathbed conversion brought me into an even deeper awareness of God's grace and His faithfulness to those who persevere in prayer for the unsaved.

> *The effective, fervent prayer of a righteous man avails much.*
> — James 5:16b

As the years progressed from the time of my salvation experience, I grew in expectancy of what the Lord would do with my sacrifice:

> *I beseech you therefore, brethren, by the mercies of God, that you present your bodies a living sacrifice, holy, acceptable to God, which is your reasonable service.* — Romans 12:1

Like most new believers, I was bursting with zeal and eager to serve. I had many repeated dreams and in one of them I saw a young girl in a long white dress. She had bright amber hair

1 The Preparation

that shone like the sun and she was standing among tall dark fir trees. I pondered on the dream, but didn't quite know how to interpret it. I thought it might be a ministry to children and tucked it away in my heart, knowing that the Lord would reveal it when I was ready. Then, one evening while walking along a deserted beach in Northern Natal, South Africa, the dream came to mind again. Songs of worship filled my heart; Scriptural songs of David and Dale Garrett, a New Zealand worship team. I felt drawn to the land as the Holy Spirit whispered to me in a still small voice that I would one day live in New Zealand. However, that revelation was for an appointed time. My mission journey was to start in my home country. The Lord is gracious in giving us glimpses of the future to encourage us, but the still small voice comes softly and gently, and one has to listen carefully so as not to miss it.

Fully convinced that I served a faithful God who would give me the desires of my heart,[4] I poured out my requests to Him in prayer: I wanted to see people come to the Lord and to experience revival in a foreign land; like the Welsh revival in 1904, and the Hebrides revival in 1949. And I longed to visit the places of the Old Testament and walk the paths that Jesus once walked.

Inspired by all the books I was reading at that time: Hudson Taylor's *China Inland Mission;* the adventures of Gladys Aylward, who rescued nearly a hundred orphaned children from lives of terror in the mountainous regions of China; and Jackie Pullinger, *Chasing the Dragon,* who rescued hundreds of youths from the drug-lords of Hong Kong, I yearned for adventure. I envisioned being a missionary and serving in China, so I prayed the prayer of offering from Isaiah chapter 8: *"Here am I! Send me!"*

No door opened, and for good reason. China was under communist rule with a policy of eliminating all religions.

Although the religious policy became more relaxed towards the late 1970s, tolerance of Christian churches came under the principles of the "Three-Self Patriotic Movement." These principles still apply today and are explained in chapter nine.

Missions Starts at Home

The mission fields were ripe in my own land, and as China was not yet an option, I sought the Lord on how I could serve at home. The small burgeoning town where I lived on the east coast of Northern KwaZulu-Natal was destined to flourish, and so were all the newly planted churches. Knowing that new churches come with fresh enthusiasm, I called them and enquired about their outreaches. One church was organizing teams to visit the sick at home, while another was training disciples for door-to-door evangelism. Others were visiting bus stops and taxi ranks to hand out gospel tracks, and planning monthly trips to rural hospitals. I asked them all if I could join in; they were delighted and didn't mind that I wasn't a member. It was on these precious outreaches that we experienced the signs and wonders that so often accompany the preaching of the Good News.

First Things First—Get Involved

Getting involved helped boost my confidence and overcome my fears. For our evangelism outreach, we approached people with a questionnaire on spiritual thinking. We always went out in teams of three and I always hid behind my two companions when it came to knocking on doors. Then one night they decided it was time I did the talking. So, on our next house visit, when the door opened, they both stepped aside and left me to face a very large man. I quickly looked from one team member to the other. They simply smiled and waited for me to speak.

***1** The Preparation*

I nervously introduced myself and our team to the man and then posed the opening questions, and to my surprise, we were invited in. My team members took a seat at the far end of the room and watched as I stumbled over my words to explain our visit. It turned out that the poor man had recently lost his wife and needed encouragement. When I realized how trivial my fears were in comparison to what others were suffering, I was able to minister to the man and even pray for him. Once I had learned to shift my focus from myself to the needs of others, I was free to be of help to those I was sent. These outreaches prepared me for a future counselling ministry.

How Will They Know Unless Someone Tells Them?

We prayed with the sick and the lonely and even with hardened atheists. We would often be surprised to see them in church the following Sunday, and their families along with them. At the taxi ranks and bus stops, we sang between the cars and buses and proclaimed the name of Lord—this chased the sangomas (witchdoctors) away and gave us a chance to share the real Good News. There was always someone who would listen and allow us to pray for them. No work for the Lord was ever wasted.

These Signs Will Follow

One day, while ministering in song at a hospital in the rural areas of Zululand, a little boy got up and danced. Loud cries rang out from the nurses and they never settled down even after the praise and worship came to an end. When we asked what the excitement was about, we were told that the little boy, still dancing, was lame from birth. Although Mark 16:17 tells us: *These signs will follow those who believe.* It's always a lovely surprise when it happens.

On another occasion, we visited a mission hospital on the top of a mountain in the Northern most parts of Zululand. Patients had to be airlifted, as the road up was too dangerous for an ambulance. There was no airlift for us; we had to drive our cars on the treacherous rocky road carved out of the mountainside, praying all the way. In places, the road was barely wide enough for a vehicle and we would teeter on the edge looking down on the sheer drop into the valley below. Once at the top, we were so grateful to have made it up alive, we did whatever was asked of us without hesitation. We worked on asbestos roofs in the sweltering African heat, painted the mission pastor's home and shared the Good News in the little village. One Saturday evening we visited the mission hospital where we prayed for a terminally ill man who had been bed ridden for six months. On Sunday morning I was to bring the message at the hospital chapel. I will never forget looking down at the smiling face of the man we had prayed for as he sat triumphantly in the front row. He was excited to tell us that he had walked to church on his own. What a mighty God we serve!

> *For since the beginning of the world men have not heard nor perceived by the ear, nor has the eye seen any God besides You, who acts for the one who waits for Him. You meet him who rejoices and does righteousness, who remembers You in Your ways.*
> — Isaiah 64:4-5

This was my mission training, and during those early years, I married and was blessed with three beautiful daughters. While the children were very young I had to give up the weekly outreaches, as it wasn't safe to take them along, but once the girls started school, I was able to work with the teams again until the political unrest of the early 1990s made it too dangerous and we had to stop altogether.

1 The Preparation

Going Through the Fire

Our outreaches were often under threat of attack. We never disregarded those warnings; we would always pray and fast and seek the Lord. One Saturday morning, the pastor of a rural church we had planned to visit called us to tell us that he had received a threat from a tribal gang. He was told that his church would be burnt down with everyone in it if we were to attend. The pastor said we were still welcome, but it was our choice whether we came or not. We fasted and prayed, and the Scripture that came to me was from Zechariah 13 verse 9.

> *I will bring the one-third through the fire, will refine them as silver is refined, and test them as gold is tested. They will call on My name, and I will answer them. I will say, "This is My people"; and each one will say, "The Lord is my God."*

Two thirds of our team had chosen not to go, but the Scripture gave me peace that we would be protected. There were only three of us who left for the village that Sunday morning. When we arrived at the little prefab school they used for their services, the pastor informed us that two-thirds of his congregation had not turned up either. Suddenly, the reality of the situation struck me; this was no idle threat. The pastor called everyone to pray and we lay face down on the floor. The fear that gripped me at that point was something I had never experienced before, and thankfully, never again—the fear of being burnt alive. Lying on the dirty wooden floor, I quickly assessed our situation. It was an old prefabricated school building made from hardboard with an asbestos roof and loose wiring hanging from the ceiling. A quick dousing of petrol and one match was all that was needed to consume the whole place in just a few minutes. Focusing on the situation in a time of dire distress was not helpful—fear overcame me. I lay there listening to the prayers of the others and holding fast to

Zechariah 13:9 in the hopes that this was just a test of faith and not a baptism of fire—there were three little girls waiting for me at home. The minutes seemed like hours and then the Lord broke the tension.

A very large lady wearing a wide-brimmed hat covered in flowers, picked up a battered guitar and walked up to the front. She placed her guitar on the table, leaned over it to support herself, and then proceeded to play. She knew only a few English words, but she sang them with gusto in an American accent. All I could make out was, *'Ya gotta have a hot line to heaven!'* All at once, everyone saw the humour in the situation and fear was replaced with joy.

He who sits in the heavens shall laugh; the Lord shall hold them in derision. — Psalm 2:4

After the song, we were able to continue the morning service peacefully, and at the end of the service, when we stepped out of the little building, we found the whole area deserted. The usual hustle and bustle of the village was stilled. We thought it best to leave immediately. We learned later that those who threatened us did come to the village, but they didn't come close to the little school. We can't be certain as to what stopped them from carrying out their threat. They may have been confused seeing the windows open on all sides, but no one on the inside as we were all face-down on the floor. And then there was the noise of the prayers that went out like a roar from this seemingly empty building that would have sounded very strange to on lookers, or perhaps they saw the angels standing guard. We'll never know, but we do know that God is faithful and when He gives us peace to go forward, we should keep our eyes on the call and not on the situation.

1 The Preparation

A New Beginning

In the later part of the 1990s, my marriage came to an end; however, I chose to see this change as a new beginning. Although my husband had, at one time, attended church, he never shared my passion for missions. The Lord never forces anyone to follow Him. We have a daily choice to obey His leading, or to choose our own way. I was pre-warned through dreams, and in one of my dreams, my husband approached me and asked for a divorce. I heard the Lord's voice saying: "Let him go." Two weeks later the dreams came to pass exactly as I had seen them. The Scriptures gave me solace that I was not out of the will of God.

> *But if the unbeliever departs, let him depart; a brother or a sister is not under bondage in such cases. But God has called us to peace.* — 1 Corinthians 7:15

However, knowing the stigma attached to divorcees in church, my hope in fulfilling my purpose and calling began to dwindle. During my divorce proceedings I became ill and needed minor surgery. One afternoon, while recovering in hospital, I looked up to see a man walking through the doorway straight towards me. We had never met before, but he assured me that the Lord had told him to come to the hospital that morning and bring me a message of hope. He prayed for me, and after he left I found a Scripture verse on my bedside table.

> *The Lord will perfect that which concerns me; Your mercy, O Lord, endures forever; do not forsake the works of Your hands.* — Psalm 138:8

Hope again rekindled, for God honours those who honour Him (John 12:26). The Lord would fulfill His purposes for me regardless of the circumstances.

After I was discharged from the hospital, a friend told me of a course she had heard about on inner-healing and deliverance with Oasis Ministries. I considered the cost in time and money of another year-long program when I had already started a thesis on Counselling for a two-year Master's degree. As no single course can cover everything on any given subject, and I felt that an additional programme could prove very useful, I prayed for the Spirit's leading. I appreciate that God uses people differently, and the way He directs me may not be the same way He guides others.

I sent for the course outline, and then prayed for wisdom before purchasing a certain book on inner-healing. When the course details arrived, I checked the book requirements, and found the book I had just purchased on the list. This leading through my book selections happened four times—too many to be a coincidence.

The new course also covered marriage and divorce, and when it arrived I approached it with a little apprehension. Even though the Lord's hand was over my life, the sting of condemnation from others often pierced through. The section on divorce was at the end of the course, which meant I would only need to tackle it months later, so I put my concerns aside and focused on the teachings. When the "dreaded subject" finally came around, I was surprised to find the study liberating with no condemnation at all. Thanks to Oasis Ministries, and Dr. Sarel Van der Merwe's balanced Biblical views, I was able, later, to teach on marriage and divorce myself.

I knew as long as I stayed focused on God's Word and not on what others were saying, I would be able to maintain my peace, and it didn't take long before new doors were opening to ministry. Once again, people asked me if divorcees could remarry or serve in a leadership capacity in the church. Divorcees are often the most hurting and misunderstood people in a

1 The Preparation

fellowship. My answer is to give your life whole-heartedly to serving the Lord and allow Him to lead you in all things. Each person's situation is different and cannot be generalized. If a fellowship holds you in bondage, leave it and find another one.

Therefore if the Son makes you free, you shall be free indeed.
— John 8:36

My masters required a full year practicum, which meant "case studies." One of the pastors in town heard I needed a room to work from and offered me an office that was not in use at his church. The condition was that I would make myself available to counsel his congregation. What an answer to prayer—I didn't have to go looking for people to complete my practicum. For the rest of that year I focused on the needs of others and grew in strength through the Word of God.

The generous soul will be made rich, and he who waters will also be watered himself. — Proverbs 11:25

The Lord proved faithful in my call and used me to save many marriages, and help those that could not be saved through the painful process of divorce. God truly does work all things together for good for them who love Him and are called according to His purposes (Romans 8:28). He doesn't waste our talents and experiences. He sent the depressed, the bereaved, the lonely, and those who were struggling with their faith. He sent children: the abused, the runaways and the broken hearted, and yes, even children battling with depression. I soon learned who the real counsellor was, and it wasn't me. I watched as the Holy Spirit touched the lives of people bringing healing and peace to their hearts. At times I would have leaders assist me in the more difficult cases, especially with those who came out of satanic cults.

Africa is rife in witchcraft. Many believers still hold to the idea that witchcraft and sorcery are archaic and should be filed away with myths and legends. Believers would often be targeted by sangomas (witch doctors), who frequently placed fetishes at their front door. Prayer and fasting would bring this activity to a halt. Some believers were of the opinion that one had to dabble in the occult, or take drugs before they could be exposed to demonic spirits, and they failed to protect themselves from open doors of heavy rock music, occultic books, and demonic movies. One mother shared with me how playing with certain toys changed her daughter's behaviour. On occasions we were asked to pray in homes where parents were experiencing continuous rebellion in their teenagers, only to find that heavy metal music or satanic books had been brought into the house. Let us not become too sophisticated for the spiritual realm. The devil still prowls around like a roaring lion looking for someone to devour. [5]

The pastor of the church where I was counselling approached me about training some of his leaders in the ministry, and so I set out to write a course on inner-healing and deliverance. I'm very grateful to the Lord for having kept me so busy while adjusting to life as a single mother, with little time to focus on the difficulties that often accompany such a radical change, especially during a time of dire political unrest. We had danger all around us as homes were regularly broken into and young girls frequently attacked

My two older daughters were away at college, and one was at a Technikon where protesters tried to sabotage the future of the students through threats and assaults in the effort to get them to quit. The police were often called out to quell the unrest. My daughter bravely stood her ground, refusing to allow anyone to rob her of her destined career even though she was accosted twice and one time at knifepoint. The Lord brought us safely through, I know we would never have managed without Him.

1 The Preparation

Leave Your Home and Your Country

I later joined a local Christian ministry pioneering part-time Bible schools for adults, and worked enthusiastically: marketing, teaching, administrating, coordinating outreaches and family counselling. The ministry work was rewarding in itself, but my efforts were not always appreciated. The enemy in the church, can, at times be more destructive than the enemy without if one is not careful. I would get bullying phone calls, emails, and confrontations from pastors and leaders who believed it their divine calling to maintain the order of a "male only" leadership in the body of Christ. What helped in those times was the knowledge that I did not seek the ministry, it came to me, and when God opens a door, no man can close it.[6]

The Lord was gracious and kept encouragement coming through a few Godly pastors and leaders, but no one told me about "burnout." It wasn't mentioned in any one of my study courses, or the numerous books I had read. It wasn't the amount of work that depleted me, I enjoyed my work, and hard work in itself never killed anyone, but rather the difficulties I had to endure *while* working was what compounded the situation. This included raising my own support, dealing with continual acts of sabotage from the enemy to destroy all my efforts, and the emotional burden of a broken family that needed healing. My three daughters had to come to terms with the divorce in their own time and with two of them away at college in different towns, plus the frequent drama of protest and attacks on students, didn't make it easy. Trusting God in these situations stretches one's faith, but keeping communication open is vital. It's the life-blood of any relationship and allows healing to flow. God's grace surrounded us, and His peace paved our pathway forward.

Then one day, after six years of pioneering work and deteriorating health, Genesis 12:1 sprang out at me.

Get out of your country, from your family and from your father's house.

And, just as Abraham was called, no direction was given. I had certainly grown from the experience of working in the Bible schools, and it was going to serve me well for years to come. By then my daughters had all married and I was free to pursue my calling. I found myself thinking of China again, and wondered if that was where God was leading me. News on the struggles and persecutions of the missionaries were frequent from various sources, and it left me doubting whether I would be able to meet the challenges of living in a communist society. All one can do in that situation is to pray and then leave it in the Father's loving hands. The Lord makes all things clear in His time, and when He calls He also equips (Hebrews 13:21).

I shared with my class that I felt a stirring within my spirit to leave my country. We discussed Genesis 26 where God instructed Abraham to worship on Mount Moriah, and using the principle of "First Mention" (a hermeneutics tool), we agreed that the essence of worship was "obedience" and "sacrifice" confirmed in Romans 12:1-2.

In the weeks that followed, I handed over my tasks to willing hands and assisted them to prepare for the next season. Right after the final graduation ceremony, I went home. I needed to be alone and seek the Lord. I remember praying quite fervently that night for direction—faith is sorely tested in the waiting.

I felt that what was about to happen would be permanent and I was never to return to live in my home country again. That night, in a dream, I saw the Lord. He appeared in a bright light. His hair shone like gold in the glow, and I wanted to reach out and touch it. No words were spoken and it lasted only a few

1 The Preparation

moments. When I awoke in the morning, I pondered on the vision and discussed it with a friend.

"Did you get your answer?" she asked, "Are you going to China?"

"I don't know," I replied, "I didn't think to ask, the vision was so peaceful there was no need for any questions." I wondered if that was how it was going to be in heaven; all the questions that we think we need answering won't matter when we're in the Lord's presence. Enveloped in the peace of God I had no remembrance of anything negative or hurtful, no unmet need and no complaint.

I opened by Bible to Hosea:

Therefore, behold, I will allure her, will bring her into the wilderness, and speak comfort to her. I will give her her vineyards from there, and the Valley of Achor a door of hope. She shall sing there, as in the days of her youth, as in the day when she came up from the land of Egypt. — Hosea 2:14-15

Although the Scripture referred to Israel, I felt there was something deeper in the meaning. I would store it within my heart throughout my journey and wait for the revelation.

Whilst continuing in prayer for the way to be made clear, the Lord directed me through another dream. This time it was England, and I was giving my Bible to a young Muslim woman. A few days later, I received a call from a friend in Scotland; she wanted me to visit and offered to pay my airfare. A door had opened. This was the start of a long, but carefully mapped out journey in a walk of faith, but most importantly on the faithfulness of God, as He fulfilled all previous prayers.

River Spey

2
Rivers of Living Waters

The work of righteousness will be peace, and the effect of righteousness, quietness and assurance forever.

Isaiah 32:17

*M*Y FIRST TRIP TO THE HIGHLANDS in Scotland was to the little town of Aviemore in the Cairngorms National Park. It was there that I dreamed once again, more than twenty years later, of the little girl with bright amber hair. She was standing among the tall fir trees just as before. This time when I awoke, I felt it was more than a ministry, it was a coming revival that would bring the church into a closer walk with her Lord.

My trip was only for a month, but it proved fruitful. I was able to start the process for a UK work visa.

My first stop the following year was Salisbury in England. I immediately sought a church and to my surprise met up with friends from South Africa. One contact leads to another and on a trip down to Bournemouth I met a South African lady involved in a ministry to aid Jews from the Ukraine to Israel. She shared with me how the Lord gave her the Russian language without having to learn it. She supernaturally began to speak Russian after praying to God for help. It was great to meet my fellow missionaries out in the world and living by the Word of Faith.

I travelled on to a quaint hamlet in Summerset and sought out the local "Bed & Breakfast" but found the local church instead. No matter where you go in the world believers are family and are always ready to welcome you. A couple in the fellowship had a ministry of hospitality and kept a room for Christian travellers. They were delighted to have me stay and sign my name in their visitor's book—they had never had a South African guest before. I was surprised to see how the Lord had honoured their ministry. Believers from all over the world had passed through this pretty little corner of England, and by divine appointment had met up with this gracious couple. Again, one contact led to another, and I was invited to stop over in Huddersfield in the heart of England, on my way north. Divine appointments are regular occurrence for those who walk by faith, and they serve to inspire and encourage us on our journey.

It was on my way North that I met a young Muslim lady in the Cotswold. She told me, quite emphatically, that no one could be certain about going to heaven. I turned to 1 John 5:13 and read it out aloud:

> *These things I have written to you who believe in the name of the Son of God, that you may know that you have eternal life, and that you may continue to believe in the name of the Son of God.*

"I want to read it myself," she said. I handed her my Bible. She read it quietly and then looked up at me. "I want to read the *whole* Bible!" She exclaimed, and so I gave her mine.

When I arrive in Huddersfield, I shared my dream of giving my Bible to a young Muslim lady and of how the dream came to pass.

2 Rivers of Living Water

"You can't travel without a Bible!" my host responded, and went off to find me one. On my next trip to Scotland, I met another new believer who did not own a Bible, and once again, handed over mine. My trip became one of giving and receiving Bibles—there is no greater gift!

I found the topography and history of the United Kingdom intriguing, and I was happy to continue there until the Lord opened another door. For the next three years, I would travel the country for nine months and return home for three to visit with my family, which was growing: two grandsons were born to my oldest daughter and a third to the second daughter; the blessings were multiplying at both ends of the world. To assist with my travel expenses, I took on part-time work as a relief carer (caregiver) attending to the needs of others: cooking, bathing and shopping, but most of all listening to their stories, and I learned something from all of them. The youngest in my care was a quadriplegic, who had lost the use of his limbs in an accident in his final year of college. I saw the raw resolve of the human spirit as he displayed courage and determination to live purposefully despite his limitations. There was a young executive whose life was unexpectedly struck down by multiple sclerosis in the height of her career, and a stroke victim who was forced into an early retirement. And the aged and lonely who thought they would live forever in a happy retirement only to be shocked into reality when their spouse was taken from them. It made me appreciate the gift of life and good health and how fragile both can be, something I will never take for granted.

You do not know what will happen tomorrow. For what is your life? It is even a vapor that appears for a little time and then vanishes away. — James 4:14

I was grateful for the freedom to live independently and also for the opportunity to serve others in a more personal capacity. Effective leaders in the Kingdom of God need to be the servants of all (Matt. 3:11). I was not permitted to share my beliefs with any of the clients, but there was nothing in my contract about friends and family. I shared the Good News with those who came to visit or work in the house and garden and they would often assure me that I was sent for them.

One of the gardeners I talked to had recently lost his father and wanted to know more about eternal life, another was a ninety-one year old lady who only knew of Jesus as a Jewish teacher in history. She was so intrigued by the Gospel story that she invited me out to lunch to hear more. She said she could not make a decision until all her questions were answered. When I replied that I didn't think she had time for all her questions, she needed to be saved now and ask questions later, she laughed and said she would definitely give it some serious thought. I never had another opportunity to talk to her, but I know that every time we share the Goods News, seeds are planted and the Lord is able to work with just a mustard seed of faith.

My travels spanned the length and breadth of England and most of Wales and Scotland—traversing hidden hinterlands and hamlets and learning of the legends that had been passed down the generations. The many hours of scenic hikes, train rides, and ferry crossings allowed my mind to rest as I continued on my journey. From the farmlands of beautiful Somerset in the south, around the picturesque Lake Districts of Cumbria, across the northwest parts of the rolling Yorkshire dales to the cold Northumberland hills and along the ruins of an ancient Roman garrison near Hadrian's Wall that divides England and Scotland, I witnessed the faith of believers who worshiped in little stone chapels with open doors to everyone. This was in stark contrast to the futility of pagans who performed rituals around the many stone circles that dotted the English countryside and who clearly did not welcome visitors.

I talked to people along the way about their church and their vision for revival, but sadly, not many were open to spiritual encounters. The Christian bookshops were places where I could learn about the spiritual climate among the believers of that town. On one such occasion I talked to the owner of a small bookshop in the North of England and he told me how they were moving in the ministry of inner-healing and deliverance in his fellowship. He said it was very seldom accepted in the local churches, but so greatly needed. I was encouraged to hear that there were believers who were experiencing a deeper conviction towards holiness and that the Holy Spirit was moving to deliver and sanctify His people.

God's plan for our lives is part of a much bigger picture, not for our personal success on earth, but for the culmination of His Church and Bride for Christ, and the preparation of the Bride, is to holiness:

But as he who called you is holy, you also be holy in all your conduct, because it is written, "Be holy, for I am holy."
— 1 Peter 1:15-16

And to righteousness:

"Let us be glad and rejoice and give Him the glory, for the marriage of the Lamb has come, and his wife has made herself ready." And to her it was granted to be arrayed in fine linen, clean and bright, for the fine linen is the righteous acts of the saints.
— Revelation 19:7-8

Inner-healing and deliverance clear the way towards these two goals.

Up to Orkney

From the northern tip of Scotland, I took a ferry to the Orkney Islands where I met up with a young friend from South Africa. Belinda was doing some illustrations for me for a children's book I was writing about inner healing, and we decided to meet up in Stromness, one of Orkney's quaint little towns. It was nice to have a travelling companion after months of going solo.

Our trek across the largest of the islands led us to the ancient Neolithic settlement of Skara Brae, uncovered by a storm in 1850. The settlement dated back to 3,200 B.C.—older than the pyramids of Egypt. We marvelled at the tenacity of man for survival in such harsh climatic conditions on the sparse island.

There was a lot of talk in the town about a Stone Age tomb dating back 5,000 years. Just like Skara Brae, it was discovered by chance in 1958, full of human bones and eagle talons. We were curious, so Belinda and I took a bus to Saint Margaret's Hope, then got a lift with a local artist to the Ronaldsay Cliffs where we went in search of the tombs. A tomb was open for viewing, but we had to crawl in. Once inside we found we could stand upright. Besides a few human skulls in a glass case, the tomb had been emptied. The story goes that the early occupants of the island offered up their dead to the sea eagles (now extinct) to feed off. When the bones were picked clean, they were placed in the tombs. It's not certain if the early settlers fed the eagles with their dead because they feared them, or because they worshiped them, but what was clear to me was that this was once a melancholy place, without Christ and *without* hope. The only person I got to witness to was a local artist who gave us a lift on our way.

2 Rivers of Living Water

Vikings, Martyrs, and Monolithic Cathedrals

A giant Viking Cathedral towered above the little town of Kirkwall, the capital of the Orkney Islands and the most northerly cathedral in the United Kingdom. You could see the sandstone structure long before the town came into view. Saint Magnus was built in 1137 A.D. to honour the holy Norse Earl of Orkney, a Viking who had converted to Christianity and was then executed for refusing to fight in a Viking raid. Christianity had reached the northern islands during the Pictish era, but it took another four hundred years for the Gospel to reach the home of the Vikings in Norway with the blood of martyrs paving the way. It saddened me to learn of yet another needless death of a believer. There have been so many throughout the ages who have suffered this fate—often in a very cruel manner. It started with the murder of Abel (Genesis 4) and escalated rapidly at the inception of the church. The twentieth century saw more Christians killed than all the centuries since the Cross, and now in the twenty-first century, the massacre of believers continues to increase. Some questions cannot be answered or understood in this life. One such question is about martyrdom. Revelation chapter 6 speaks of a number of martyrs destined for the altar in heaven:

> When He opened the fifth seal, I saw under the altar the souls of those who had been slain for the word of God and for the testimony which they held. And they cried with a loud voice, saying, "How long, O Lord, holy and true, until You judge and avenge our blood on those who dwell on the earth?"
> Revelation 6:9-10

I do not feel that this Scripture allows the church to be complacent about persecution. Revival is needed and it could prevent a number of untimely deaths.

Clowns of the Sea

Another short ferry trip from Kirkwall took us to Westray, a smaller island in Orkney's archipelago, just north of the Mainland. Our goal was to find "puffins." I promised myself that I wasn't leaving Orkney without seeing one. We asked a local farmer where they nested and he pointed us in the direction, but told us that it was too early in the season; the puffins would still be out at sea. Seeing a puffin was one of the reasons I visited Orkney, and I knew I wouldn't be returning that way again, so I was determined to find one.

"Please, Lord, send the puffins in to land," we were praying out loud as we cycled along the edges of the wind-blown cliffs to where the birds would come in to nest.

Belinda saw one first, but hesitated to say, as she wasn't sure if it was a puffin. Then I shouted out: "Thank you Lord!" They were flying in fast and furious.

We watched as they dropped on the cliff-top, running along with a wobble, struggling to balance their little stout bodies before coming to a final halt. I could see why the locals found them amusing; with their large orange beaks and big rounded feet, they did look like little clowns. It felt good to be out amongst nature and away from the tragic history of mankind.

Cycling from one end of Westray to the other, and back, allowed us a few minutes on our return before the evening Arctic winds made it too difficult to ride at all. We pushed our bikes to the farm where we had hired them, then walked down to wait for the ferry to take us to the Mainland. We certainly had our fill of adventure, with history, archaeology, and ornithology to complete the day.

2 Rivers of Living Water

Belinda's Story

Belinda had recently graduated with a degree in biochemistry from a university in South Africa. She fell in love with the highlands and wanted to remain in the UK to fulfill her dream in combining her studies in chemistry with sports research. The biggest hurdle, though, was in the tuition costs. One of the universities that accepted her had kindly deferred her application for a year while she went in search of finances.

"Seek first the Kingdom of God," the Scriptures instruct us (Matt. 6:33), so we committed it into the Lords loving hands while Belinda later returned to South Africa and waited for a door to open. God proved faithful and made a way for her to pay the tuition without having to incur debt.

Ephesians 3:20 tells us that God is able to do *exceedingly, abundantly above all that we ask or think, according to the power that works in us*. Not only could Belinda complete her Masters in pharmacology in the UK, the university also had a sports department with altitude simulating facilities. They structured a project for her on sports medical research, fulfilling her dream. Needless to say, she scored as one of the top in the class with a distinction.

Ministry of Monks

Twice I visited a place that really stirred my spirit. Inchcolm Island in Scotland is not very well known to tourists, but to the locals it's the "Iona of the East." This little Isle is located in the middle of the Firth of Forth (the bay where the River Forth empties into the North Sea). It is four miles east of the Forth Bridge in Edinburgh, the capital city of Scotland—just a short ferry ride. The origin of Christianity on Inchcolm is shrouded in mystery. No one lives on this island now. The Abbey stands as a ghostly reminder of its lonely past inhabitants. I never got to speak to anyone, but I felt the Abbey speaking to me. It was built around 1,200 A.D. for the Augustinian monks. The exact date is uncertain, but before the monks arrived, the Island was inhabited by "holy hermits" who lived saintly lives in isolated cells (small stone buildings). They named the Island after Saint Columba, a feisty Irish monk who started a war in Ireland and was duly banished to Iona, an Island on the west coast where he established a monastery in his mellowing years. "Commitment to holiness and dedication to the call" was the message I received whilst exploring the empty chambers. Although this tiny island was a haven of peace and tranquillity, it is often the target of gale force winds that race through the bay from off the North Sea. As I walked down the drafty cloisters of the Abbey, I shuddered at the thought of the icy North winds cutting through every crack and crevice of the uninsulated walls and roof. In the chapter house, the monks would sit on stone benches, painstakingly copying the Scriptures by hand, regardless of the weather. The walls of the chapter house had large openings that looked out to the sea with no hint as to how they were secured on a stormy night. The monks could warm themselves in "The Warming House," a large room with a fireplace, and on the wall are words inscribed in Latin:

It is foolish to fear what cannot be avoided. The safest thing is to fear nothing but God.

What a message for us today in our materialistic and fast-paced technological world.

The monastery was so alluring that I had to return the following year. However, my second visit wasn't as peaceful. I decided to walk to the end of the west side to see if any puffins had come in to roost. This part of the island is home to a large colony of gulls and arctic terns who don't welcome visitors. I was forewarned by the guide who ferried across every day, and

2 Rivers of Living Water

then further warned by the birds themselves with a cacophony of cries. My punishment, for not paying heed, was a blasting from the bowels of the terns as they opened fire down the side of my new jacket. I wondered how many monks had suffered the same fate, having had to share such a small piece of real estate in the Firth of Forth.

Shifting Sands of Time

Each year I would return to my family in South Africa for the Christmas season, and then back to the UK, hoping that this would be the year of revival. On my third return to England, in 2007, my three daughters decided to emigrate: one had applied to Australia and the other two were looking towards New Zealand. They called and asked if I would like to join them. I had to decide whether to remain in the UK permanently, or return to South Africa and prepare to emigrate with them. Either way, the doors to my home country in South Africa were closing, permanently.

Remembering my walk on the beach in Northern Natal when I was still a very new believer, and the prompting I felt towards New Zealand. I felt the shifting sands of my itinerant life were moving me towards my final destiny.

Rivers of Living Water

In a church in the small town of Linlithgow near Edinburgh, I was told of a man who had witnessed the Hebrides Revival in the 1940s. He believed that he would live to see the next one, but my time in the UK was running out. I returned to Aviemore, the place I visited when I first arrived; this would be my last visit to Scotland. I climbed the hills near the Cairngorm Mountains in the hopes that the Lord would speak to me there. In South Africa, I loved to walk on the plateaus of the Drakensburg Mountain Range. There is something about the silence of the quiescent mountains with their jagged peaks that draws one to take cognizance of our mighty creator. We can be close to the Lord in the valleys too, but the mountains have a special appeal to me.

I looked out towards the giant white crests of the Cairngorms and waited. The hours passed and all was quiet without and within. The sound of bagpipes filtered up through the trees. The skirl of the pipes filled my senses as though calling me back down. The pipers would play in the town square in the afternoon, attesting to the beauty and uniqueness of this extraordinary land. I would see the piper for the last time and hurried on down the rough trail to the valley below. My piper turned out to be a recording playing from the camping site. Another disappointment in the day, or what appeared to be. The Lord often speaks when we least expect it, when we relinquish expectation.

I made my way down to the River Spey and stepped off the bank onto a large stone in the shallow, still part of the water. I watched as the river flowed continuously and forcefully, but most of all, effortlessly.

He who believes in Me, as the Scripture has said, out of his heart will flow rivers of living water. — John 7:38

Effortlessly was the key. When ministry flows out of worship, it allows the Spirit to work apart from the flesh; continuously, forcefully, and effortlessly just like the river. The Lord will visit those who are worshipping in spirit and in truth. I prayed a silent prayer that I could return if an outpouring of the Spirit should visit there.

Usk Castle Gate

3
When All Doors Close

Stand in the ways and see, and ask for the old paths, where the good way is, and walk in it; then you will find rest for your souls.

Jeremiah 6:16

WHEN MY TWO YOUNGER DAUGHTERS and their families left for New Zealand, I stayed behind in South Africa to help my eldest daughter with her final arrangements for her emigration to Australia. Once the families in New Zealand had settled, I flew over. I was not able to acquire a resident visa and had to enter New Zealand on a visitor's visa with a nine-month extension. I felt confident that it would be enough time for a door to open to secure my stay, so I joined a local church and on occasions, served at the training centre as a guest lecturer. I felt right at home teaching discipleship, worship and New Testament studies. However, when my visa expiration date approached, my hope of remaining in New Zealand began to dwindle. I held on fast in faith that something would turn up at the eleventh hour; after all, this was where I was destined to be.

The church I was attending could sponsor me as a missionary, but I would have had to raise my own support, *without* a New Zealand work permit. Immigration advised me that I would have to wait another three years before I could be sponsored on a parent visa, and then there could be a further two-year wait once the application was submitted. The door was slowly closing. I was confused and becoming increasingly anxious; I would soon be without a home and country. I called immigration again.

"Apply for a student visa," the immigration officer tried to sound hopeful. A student visa required a letter from an academic institute, so I called one of the language schools. TEFL (Teach English as a Foreign Language) classes were only held if there were enough people to warrant it, and there weren't. I would have to wait for the next course. I called another school, but they were not offering the course I needed—the door kept closing. The Lord was leading me out, but where was I to go? The next day, I received an email from New Zealand immigration. I had to exit the country in less than four weeks. My fingers raced fervently across the keyboard as I searched the internet and prayed all the while: *"Lord, open a door, open a door!"*

A friend called me to tell me that an international language school in Prague, Czech Republic was open for more candidates and they guaranteed jobs after training. I phoned the school to confirm and explained my situation. I was assured that there were plenty of jobs in Prague and I would get hundreds of contacts to pursue while on the course. Most importantly, I had peace to go; not because of a man's promise, but because of God's promise, that He would guide me in every situation. I felt an urgency to move on.

The next thing was to apply for a Schengen visa to enter the Czech Republic and the embassy was in Australia. I called them and once again explained my situation. They were very

3 When All Doors Close

helpful and sent me all the documentation via email. I was to courier the papers to Australia, and, providing everything was in order, they would process the visa as soon as possible. I sent off my passport and papers and booked my flight in faith that my passport would be returned in time. My visa was granted two weeks before my departure. I left for Prague on 28th February 2009, sad and confused that the door to New Zealand had closed on me. I have learnt ever since, that when all doors close and I feel as though I'm standing in an empty hallway, to praise the Lord, His timing is always perfect and He does considerably more than we can ever hope or imagine. Oblivious to the adventures that lay ahead, and that I was finally going to China that very same year, I rested in the promise that: *All things work together for good to those who love God, to those who are the called according to His purpose* (Romans 8:28).

Tyn Church

4
Prague

And I will betroth you to Me in faithfulness, and you shall know the Lord.

Hosea 2:20

IT FELT COMFORTABLE TO BE back at Heathrow Airport, seeing all the familiar shops and finding my way around the terminal. I walked past a room stacked to the ceiling with unclaimed baggage and peered in through the glass partitions. The bags all appeared to be labelled, but still unclaimed. After six months they get auctioned off. I had missed planes, trains, and buses, but never had to deal with lost luggage. I shuddered at the thought of arriving in a strange country without my belongings. To add to my fears, I had not packed a fresh change of clothes in my hand luggage. *Next time I fly,* I thought, *I won't take that for granted again, and carry the necessaries on board.* I sat down to enjoy a quick coffee, and then off to collect my boarding pass. There was just enough time to get my ticket and catch the airport bus to the next terminal.

Finally, after a 28 hour sleepless journey, I arrived in Prague, where my fears unfolded before me—no suitcase on the carousel. My quick change in flights did not allow time for baggage transfer. For peace of mind, it would have been better to have collected my case at Heathrow and checked it in myself on the connecting flight—another travel lesson noted.

The taxi took me to my apartment right in the centre of the town. Tired, *sans* luggage, or a fresh change of clothes, I decided to go for a walk to look for an exchange booth. After a few wrong turns, and feeling rather defeated, I gave up the adventure of the day and made my way back to my apartment in the hope that my luggage would arrive to greet me in the morning. It did, and once I had settled into my classes and paced myself with the work, I found that I had the weekends free to explore the city and puzzle together the fragmented pieces of my Eastern European history.

Clock Makers and Women Shapers

Prague is a small city, but it can be tricky to navigate. It once served as a trade route between Southern and Northern Europe from as early as 500 B.C. The maze of winding cobbled streets were designed to confuse marauders who were hastily trapped and quartered—no thought given to the tourists of the twenty-first century. I learnt very quickly not to look lost, as you soon become the target of local chancers wanting to pick you up.

Once through the narrow streets towards the old city, I came face to face with the 14th century town hall and the famous Astronomical Clock. I stood in awe of the huge dials and zodiacs representing its medieval view of the world with the planets circling the earth instead of the sun. A tour guide was telling the story of the clockmaker and how the king had his eyes gouged out on completion of the clock so he could never make another one like it. The clockmaker retaliated by

4 Prague

climbing up the back of the clock and sabotaging it. He put a curse on anyone who tried to fix it, and as it happened, anyone who did, subsequently died. Stories like these, and Prague is full of them, keep tourism alive in the Old Town. The clock suffered severe damage in World War II, but it was later repaired to its full function without any further tragedies.

When the guide informed us that the place where we were standing was the original site of public executions, where the reformers, Jerome and Hus were martyred in the fifteenth century, I quickly moved on. Directly opposite was the famous landmark of Tyn Church, founded by the foreign merchants of the 12th century. The present construction from the 14th century boasted of two 80-meter high, Gothic towers that loom over the Old Town Square paying tribute to the rise and fall of the Hussites (followers of Jan Hus). On the southern side of the square were the colourful palatial apartment houses, and directly in front, the memorial of John Hus who was burnt at the stake in 1415; Jerome was burnt a year later.

Prague was once the capital of the Holy Roman Empire and opposing doctrines were never tolerated. Jan Hus had bravely prepared the way for the Great Reformation later spearheaded by Martin Luther, but the real heroine for me was Ann of Bohemia.

The story of Hus' conversion to the true faith can be traced back to the marriage of a Bohemian princess to King Richard II of England. Princess Anne had a passion for the Scriptures and came to value the pure doctrines of the apostles of the early church. She sponsored students to study in England under John Wycliffe, and they, in turn, brought the teaching of Wycliffe back to Prague and Jan Hus. Hus' death birthed the Hussite Movement, and from out of the Hussite Movement came the Moravians who in turn, were instrumental in the transformation of the life of John Wesley.

All the faithful women throughout history, who influenced the generations that followed, are heroines to me. Especially the women who were divinely placed in the genealogy of Jesus:

The Egyptian princess, who turned from the Egyptian gods and embraced the God of the Hebrews, married Mered from the tribe of Judah.[7] Jewish tradition believes her to have been the princess who pulled Moses out of the Nile. Josephus refers to her as "Thermuthis." [8]

Rahab, the harlot of Jericho, who assisted the two spies of Joshua, married Salmon of Judah and became the great grandmother of King David in the genealogy of Jesus.[9]

Ruth, the Moabite, who turned to the Hebrew God and married Boaz, became the grandmother of King David.[10]

And those who followed Him without hesitation:

The Samaritan woman, whom Jesus ministered to at a well, became His first evangelist. Jesus was sent to the house of Israel,[11] yet He did not overlook the faith of this non-Jewish woman, even though in the Jewish culture of that time, Jewish men regarded their own women as inferior and *Gentile* women as deserving no regard at all. Jesus never looks at outward appearances, He can see straight into the heart. She evangelized her whole town and was rewarded for her faith; Jesus stopped over with them for two days before returning to the house of Israel. [12] This resulted in the conversion of many Gentiles even before the Cross.

Then there were the Marys: Mary the mother of Jesus; Mary the wife of Clopas, who stood faithfully by Him at the foot of the Cross, along with Mary of Magdalene who had followed Him closely, ministered to Him, washed His feet, and was the first to see Him resurrected; and Mary of Bethany, sister of Lazarus and Martha, who always sat listening at His feet, pouring perfume over them just before His death, and to

4 Prague

whom John Wycliffe compared Queen Anne of Bohemia, wife of King Richard II (the same Anne mentioned on page 49).

Martyred Monks and Kings

Prague was no ordinary city, stained with the blood of the martyrs, and yet, renowned as the Educational Mecca of Eastern Europe; Charles University being the first university to be established in Central Europe in 1348. On Charles Bridge, I paused to view the Vltava River stretching out in both directions with row upon row of lesser bridges. The giant medieval castle with its Gothic Vista Cathedral stood on the far side. I passed by artists, musicians, and puppeteers and then stopped to look up at the tall statue of a martyred monk standing right in the centre of the bridge.

Neopmonk was tortured and thrown into the river on the command of a jealous king for not revealing the queen's confession within the confinement of the church. The shrewd monk had promised the king that he would share the queen's confession on Sunday morning, but when the king returned to hear it, the monk had already shared it with his dog. The brass plates on both sides of the base of the statue shone like mirrors from the touch of the passers-by in the hopes of finding love and good fortune. The town was full of superstitions; people putting their faith in departed saints instead of the risen Lord who can save them. I was thankful that our God and King, who is a jealous God, came to save us, and not to destroy us.

Once across the bridge, the winding stairs took me up to a ninth century castle, the former residence of Good King Wenceslas I, Duke of Bohemia. He was a believer of the faith, and one of Prague's earliest martyrs; murdered on his way to church. He is remembered around the world at Christmas time in the carol "Good King Wenceslas." Tired from the excitement and information overload of the day, I returned to my apartment for an early night. The next day was Sunday; I needed to search online for a nearby fellowship and found one in walking distance from where I lived.

Trust and Obey

The next morning, I made my way to the Prague Christian Fellowship where I met Matt, who was involved with city outreach.

"There are 10,000 homeless in the Czech Republic," he informed me. "And 4 to 6 thousand of them are in Prague, mostly men between the ages of 20 and 50."

"Really?" I replied. "Why don't they get jobs?" Matt shrugged his shoulders.

"Many of them are still influenced by the old ways. They feel that the government should support them. They refuse to work."

Matt assured me that there would be plenty of work in the city and offered to connect me with Christian flat-shares.

I sat down and listened to a message on Job and how God blessed him for his obedience. It reminded me of my last message to my students at the Bible School in South Africa on Genesis 26—God blesses obedience! My thoughts fell on China. I had an uneasy feeling that doors for employment were not going to open to me in Prague. I decided I would concentrate on my studies and see as much of the city as I could before my month was up.

During my second week, I was sent to take a class at a school in the Old Jewish Quarter. I had to go through the Old Town Square, but as usual, I took the wrong turn out of the square. I've never been shy to stop and ask for directions; it's much quicker than reading outdated maps. The old quarter looked intriguing; I quickly scanned my surroundings whilst running to make it in time for my class. As soon as Saturday came around, I was up early, had breakfast and raced down the streets towards the Old Town Square. This time I had to find the right entrance to the Jewish Quarter.

The Old Jewish Quarter

It seems as though everyone in the city was up before me. Tourists were congregating in groups all over the Old Town Square waiting for tour guides. I heard someone say their group was going through the Jewish Quarter first, so I joined in behind them. The guide arrived with a red flag she used to summon her little band of sightseers when they dispersed along the way. She stopped by a large church just before entering the Jewish Quarter and relayed a tale of a medieval peasant who was caught with his hand in the offering basket. The poor lad was taken into the square and had his hand removed from his arm. Seems like the mediaeval priests of Prague had not learned the meaning of a "hyperbole," and took the words of Jesus literally. [13]

"The skeleton hand still hangs from the rafters directly over the offering basket if you'd like to go in and see it," she announced as an apex to the story. No one even shuffled. "Are you sure?" She pressed, and then raised her flag and summoned us to follow her into the old Jewish Quarter.

Thirty-one streets and lanes, twelve passages and six gates mapped out the walled ghetto of the Byzantine and Ashkenazi Jewish settlers from the 11th to the 13th centuries. The last of the gates was cancelled in 1822. In the course of centuries, the houses, streets, and synagogues grew and gave rise to the famous Jewish Academy, a Talmudic School, and a Town Hall. Our guide stopped in front of a small ordinary looking building.

"This is Pařížská Street (Paris Street)," she announced proudly. "See the beautiful buildings and how the trees line the streets between open cafes, just like Paris." The corner building to our right did look very ornate, in a true baroque style. "And behind us," she continued, "is the 13th century Old New Synagogue of Rabbi Yehuda who created the Golem, it still lies in the attic today."

The Golem? My ears pricked up. The story of the Golem started here in the Old Synagogue on Paris Street, in Prague? I had heard of the story of the Golem, but had no idea it was resting in Europe's oldest active synagogue, in the Czech Republic—another piece of my Eastern European history puzzle in place.

According to the legend, Rabbi Yehuda Ben Bezalel made a giant clay figure called Golem. It was created to protect the inhabitants of the Ghetto and could be brought to life by inserting a small tablet with a magic formula (various letters of the Hebrew alphabet) into a slot in its forehead. Of course, everyone wanted to see it, but mysterious legends cannot be so easily unveiled. Our guide proceeded to tell us why.

During the Nazi occupation of WWII, a Gestapo commander was ordered to destroy the Golem. He sent a soldier into the synagogue to get it, but as the soldier approached the stairway to the attic, he suffered a heart attack and fell upon the lower steps. The soldier was dragged out of the synagogue and the commander retreated. The floorboards and steps the soldier fell upon were removed, but the steps were never replaced. No one could reach the attic again. And so, the Golem was left to lie in peace, never to be revived, but continues to uphold the legend for all time. The red flag went up and the tour group made their way down a narrow winding street and out of the Old Quarter.

I slipped away and walked back down Paris Street. Guards stood outside the entrances of the row of synagogues to prevent tourists from wandering in. It was Shabbat and services were in progress. As I passed by, I could hear the chanters calling out in their Sabbath service. The echo of their cry sent a wave of sadness over me that I was unable to shrug off for the rest of that day.

A Call to Cappadocia

I found Prague a very difficult place to evangelize, and it wasn't because of the language barrier, many people spoke English, but they were not open to the Gospel. The city was becoming increasingly crowded. Preparations were underway for a visit from the American President. Helicopters hovered above the town for days, surveilling the nuclear protests and other marches. My final week on the course was coming to an end. The schools in the city would be employing again in September and it was only the end of March. My visa was still valid for another two months, but my finances were running low. I kept applying for work; however, no doors were opening. I felt it best to get out of town and away from the crowds while I thought about my next move. I had another option, and it was my last hope.

My brother had accepted a post in Turkey and was now teaching at a University in Ankara. I called him and asked if I could stay there for a couple of weeks while I continued my job search.

"Sure," he replied, "but I'm off to Wales on a conference next week, so you'll have to wait a week before you come over."

Another week in Prague would be too expensive, and to add to my dilemma, I was coming down with the flu. I quickly found a reasonably priced guesthouse just outside the city, right on the riverbank. It proved to be a very quiet and restful stay while I waited out my week before leaving for Turkey. No one speaks English once you're out of the city, except for the two dear ladies at the guesthouse who directed me to the local pub where I had my afternoon meals.

We were cautioned at the language school that American passport holders were advised not to enter Turkey. There was a lot of political unrest between the United States and Turkish government at that time, and to make matters worse, the American President was now on his way to Turkey! I was travelling on a South African passport, but my new suitcase had a metal label on the top that read "American Traveller." I tried to remove it, but it was secured from the inside and I would need to cut through the lining. I attempted to scratch off the writing instead, but even that proved unsuccessful. I decided to go in the faith that no one would notice it. Slashing cases was a frequent occurrence in countries that strongly objected to certain cultures.

The day before I was to leave for Istanbul, I met a dear lady coming into the breakfast room pulling a very tattered case on wheels. She sat down and proceeded to chat away in German. She had seen my name in the visitor's book and presumed I was fluent in German too. I stammered over a few words, enough to let her know that I was not.

"But you have a Swiss name?" She said with a heavy accent.

"Yes, I have a Swiss father, I'm South African," I replied.

"I'm, Swiss too," she announced, "but, it's too expensive to live there, so I travel."

She asked me where I was off to, and I told her that I was planning to leave for Turkey the following day.

"Where in Turkey?" She inquired.

"I'm going to Ankara, to visit my brother."

She thought for a moment and then exclaimed wide-eyed

as she took hold of my arm. "You must go to Kappadocia! Kappadocia!" she repeated and shook my arm.

"What's Kappdosee?" I asked.

"Kappadocia," she took out a pencil and wrote the name down on a piece of paper, spelling it with a "K" as the Swiss/Germans do. "The underground cities of the Christians." She handed me the paper.

"The what ... ?" She had my attention.

"The underground cities of the Christians and the fairy chimney." She gestured with her hands in the air, spiralling to demonstrate the chimneys. "It's the most beautiful place in the world in the spring time, and I've travelled to lots of places." She proceeded to describe the striking beauty of it all, and how the desert flowers bring the whole region to life after the spring rains. My thoughts were fixed on the underground cities of the Christians.

The little I knew about the Cappadocians was that they were among the very first to receive the baptism of the Holy Spirit on the day of Pentecost.[14] They had heard the Gospel in their own language and brought the Good News back to the land of Anatolia. She was right. I had to go to Cappadocia! I left for Istanbul the following morning with a renewed excitement. Finding work was now the last thing on my mind.

Atatürk Airport Istanbul

5
Visas and Vestibules

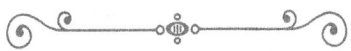

Let Patience have its perfect work ....
James 1:4

STEPPING INTO THE TRANSIT HALL in Istanbul felt more like stepping into a marketplace on a Saturday morning than an international airport. People were pushing in and out of queues to purchase entrance visas. The cost of the visas varied according to the country you came from. The New Zealanders and Australians entered freely; South Africans got the next cheapest deal, and the Swedish paid the most. I was wondering what the Swedes had done to annoy the Turks when a British businessman standing beside me began complaining about the long queues and the price he had to pay for his visa.

"This is ridiculous!" he said turning to me. "And, they don't give you enough time for a transit!" I nodded and joined in behind; I had to focus on keeping my place in the queue. I watched the clock as I waited my turn. My flight to Ankara was due to board in less than twenty minutes. At last, I was shoved towards the counter where I handed over my passport.

"Wrong queue." A voice bellowed at me from behind the window. "South Africa, over there." He pointed to an even longer line of people.

Oh, heck, I thought, *I'm really going to miss my flight now!* I pushed my way to the correct queue, thinking that if I prayed fervently enough I could hold back time a little, or hasten the process. It also helped to keep me focused.

The shoving and pushing kept us moving, and before long, I was at another window purchasing a visa. For once, I was pleased with my South African passport—I only paid 10 Euros. Relieved that I'd finally got my passport stamped, I raced to the departure gate for my next surprise. A big sign in English informed me that boarding for Ankara had been redirected to another gate, which was about to close in two minutes. I checked the screen monitors to confirm the gate number and then took off, dodging the oncoming travellers and pushing through the maddening crowds. A woman waved her arms and shouted at me.

"Sorry," I yelled back, as I ran. I scanned the terminal for a sign with directions in English finally reaching the gate, out of breath and head spinning. It was deserted, except for one lone attendant, but thankfully, still open.

The plane was parked out on the runway and the last bus was due to leave. The flight attendant clipped my boarding pass and hurried me along. I leaped on board the bus just as the doors were closing and squashed in amongst the other travellers. Holding on fast to a rail and trying to catch my breath and keep my balance at the same time, I heard a voice behind me.

"Only crazy people travel." I looked around to see the British businessman I'd met earlier, shaking his head at me and smiling.

"Yeah," I agreed, and smiled back. We boarded the plane and finally I could relax. I fell back in my seat, buckled up and waited for take-off. Tired, dehydrated, and weekend by the flu, I dreaded the customs delay on the other side. *You wanted adventure and you wanted to travel,* I told myself, *so you can't complain!* After all, it wasn't the first, nor would it be the last time I had to run for a flight.

Midnight in Ankara

It was late at night when I came through Domestic Arrivals at Ankara airport and I was in the throes of a migraine. I was expecting to arrive at the international side and so was my brother, Bernard. He had returned from Wales the previous day and he too, had the flu. Needless to say, he wasn't happy at having to be out in the cold night air. While he was waiting at International Arrivals, I was waiting in the draughty domestic lounge. It was close to midnight and the place was slowing down, soon there might be no one around. It was then I realized that I only had Bernard's home number and not his mobile. I texted family in Scotland and New Zealand to see if anyone had his mobile number, but to no avail. Then, just as I was thinking of booking into a hotel for the night, he turned up. After waiting an hour at International, he decided to check out Domestic Arrivals and found me close to tears.

We took a bus from the airport to the city; the streets were deserted. After scaling a gruelling flight of stairs on an overpass, we caught another bus to the university campus on the outskirts of town. There were another six flights of stairs to haul up my 26 kg suitcase before we finally reached his apartment. These uninteresting little expeditions are things one never forgets. We both took two days to recover.

Bernard was busy with his classes and couldn't take any more time off; he suggested I take a bus from Ankara to see some of the sites on my own. As Ephesus was a bit too far, he too suggested Cappadocia, my intended destination. He accompanied me to purchase a travel ticket and on the day of my departure, I was up earlier than usual to make sure I didn't miss my coach.

Cappadocia

6
Land of Beautiful Horses

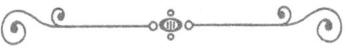

*They wandered in the wilderness in a desolate way;
they found no city to dwell in.*

Psalm 107:4

MARKET STALLS LINED THE BUSY bus terminal and the smell of hot spicy foods wafted from each side. I felt a little vulnerable being the only foreign woman in sight—it drew a lot of attention. I was thankful that I didn't have to negotiate a ticket and I could go straight to my coach. I climbed on board and took my seat. The coach was crowded and stuffy, and I was beginning to feel nauseous from the strong smell of garlic in the increasingly stifling heat. At last, the engines roared and the air-conditioner turned on. It was a four-and-a-half-hour drive into the desert. I had a window seat and turned my attention to the surrounding terrain; mile after mile of flat arid land. We were on our way to a desert after all, what could I have expected?

After two hours, we stopped for twenty-five minutes to stretch our legs, and then back on the road again. The women appeared agitated; hands were going up and something was being passed around. I was trying to see what it was when a string of large brown beans swung across my face as they were being flung backward. I leaned out of the way to avoid them hitting my nose. The passenger next to me took them, and then she cocked her head toward me.

"American!" She announced to the others in disapproval. A call resounded from the front of the bus. It was Friday noon and the midday prayer hour was to be conducted in the appropriate fashion. At first, there was silence as all heads bowed over the beads, and then, a crescendo of cries filled the bus as they uttered the customary prayer. Turkey had been a secular state since the inception of Kemalism (the founding ideology of Turkey), but Islam still ruled in every community.

We arrived in the little town of Nevşehir around 3 p.m. I was thankful to get off the coach and find my own space to breath in the hot desert air. This was a far cry from the busy streets of Prague and the bustle of Istanbul terminal. Tall white minaret towers rose above the flat roofed, stone buildings. In the stillness of the sweltering heat, I wondered what the archives of ancient empires, that once rose and fell throughout the ebb and flow of history, would reveal, if I could glimpse into their past.

I envisioned a trail of blood running through the desert from the Biblical Hittites to the assailing Assyrians; the marauding Medes to the pillaging Persians, and—not to forget—the invincible Alexander the Great. The Romans and Byzantines all had their turn before the Seljuk with their Caliphs and Sultans, and then came the Crusaders and the Ottomans. The persecution of the believers continued on into the twentieth century, escalating in WWI with the massacre of over a million Armenian Christians in fatal death marches.

Armenia was the first country to become a Christian state and they paid for it with their lives. The Arab invasion of Armenia

6 *Land of Beautiful Horses*

in the 7th century forced thousands of surviving Armenians into Turkey. During WWI, more than a million Christian Armenians were massacred, starting in Constantinople and ending in the Syrian Desert where the few survivors finally met their fate. Then it all came to an end ... or has it?

Turkey is one of the many Muslim majority countries that surround Israel and it is geographically positioned true north of Israel. [15]

In the Oracles of Ezekiel, Gomer and the house of Togarmah are from the far north.

> *Gomer and all its troops; the house of Togarmah from the far north and all its troops—many people are with you.*
>
> — Ezekiel 38:6

Ezekiel chapter 38 and 39 speak of Tubal, Togarmah, and Meshech. The Zondervan Bible Atlas sites these places in Anatolia with Togarmah on the Eastern border of Cappadocia.[16] (Togarmah was a son of Gomer, grandson of Japheth, and great-grandson of Noah - Genesis 10:3.)

Gazing down the dusty road, I thought I saw a *Gazis* (Turkish horseman) on a black stead, brandishing a sabre. The sound of a horn brought me back to reality.

Fairy Chimneys and Cave Dwellings

My next bus ride was a short one, only 10 km to Göreme. The topology changed dramatically as we descended into the semi-desert valley. The sparse, flat terrain of the plateau rose into peculiar cone shaped rocks that jutted up from every side.

Many of them had a small flat stone balancing on the top as though it had been strategically placed there. Thousands of years ago, Erciyes, a now extinct volcano, had once erupted over a two hundred kilometer range, leaving behind a ten meter deep ash-blanket that later solidified into tuff (soft rock). Hundreds of years of wind and water erosion stripped away the softer rock leaving the hard cap rock on tall pillars the locals call, "fairy chimneys." To me, they looked more like rock missiles. This area had been a location for science fiction movies.

The bus jolted us back and forth as it bounced over the rocky road. I held fast to my seat, thankful that it was just a ten-minute ride. The village had only one main street with bustling markets and restaurants. Vendors yelled at me from every side to stop and look at their intricately woven Persian carpets, all competing to offer a better deal.

"We ship back to your country," one shouted. "Price included." I shook my head and smiled. I had no country to ship back to, besides, it was late afternoon, and I only had the weekend to take in all the sights. I stopped at one of the street cafés, and then turned down a small dusty road to a cave pension nestled in the corner of the village. It was the perfect spot, right near the Göreme museum.

My room was damp and musty, what one would expect from a cave dwelling. Göreme had many of these pensions (guesthouses) hewn into the numerous sedimentary rocks across the region of Cappadocia. *Two nights,* I thought, *I can bare it.* I dropped my bags, picked up my purse and camera, and locked my door. I turned to see the pension manager beckoning me from under a table umbrella. He had sweet Turkish tea and a whole itinerary of things to do. Early morning hot air ballooning, Turkish traditional dinners, guided tours, and special deals on locally made merchandise were among them. I booked a Turkish dinner for the following night and a tour of the underground cities for the morning, but skipped the hot air ballooning—my budget didn't allow for it. He pointed me

6 Land of Beautiful Horses

in the direction of the Open Air Museum. It was a 15-minute walk, and I still had a little over an hour before closing.

The road was quiet with no one in sight. Here and there, I could see a Turkish flag flying from the top of a stone house. The fairy chimneys had served as homes for desert dwellers since the 4th century. When the tuff was wet, it became soft and easy to carve into. The strong desert winds had forged many unusual shapes out of the soft tuff, giving each house a different design. Some shapes looked like animals, some like mushrooms, while others were quite bizarre. I passed one on the right that resembled a camel looking out towards the road with a doorway cut between its legs. On the left of the road, the hills were carpeted in green with hues of yellow from the wild flowers that sprawled across them. I had come in time to witness the artistry of the spring rains.

Tall perpendicular rocks and narrow sandy pathways intercepted the green and yellow tapestry, then, to my surprise—horses! Greys, duns, and palominos were grazing peacefully on the grassy slopes. I stopped to take pictures. This was truly ancient *Katpatuka*, "Land of Beautiful Horses."

I had walked for nearly 15 minutes and all I saw before me were looming rocks. At last, someone coming from the opposite direction—he looked foreign.

"Where *is* this place?" I called, hoping he understood English and "the place" I was looking for.

"Follow the road to the right," he shouted back. The road continued to wind, the stone pillars were getting larger and higher as I walked further on. Then, around another corner and off to the right, the rocks suddenly parted. I turned onto a wide sandy pathway and stepped into a large semi-circular rocky enclosure. I stopped for a moment, surprised by the scene that transpired before me. Everywhere I looked, I saw small figures entering and exiting rectangular openings high up in the rocks.

People were climbing up and down steep rocky steps as they went from one level to the next.

The Hiding Place

This monastic village provided shelter for the early Christians from the Arab raiders and then later from the Ottomans. It was indeed well hidden from the main road and very true to its name, *Gör emi*, "you cannot see this place." What a perfect hide out for a monastic community. I paid the entrance fee, picked up an information booklet, and wandered in.

According to the booklet, I was standing in a 4th century monastic centre where Basil the Great, Bishop of Caesarea had inspired many religious colonies together with his brother Gregory of Nyssa and Gregory of Nazianzus. They went down in history as "The Cappadocia Fathers," widely known for their defence in the divinity of the Holy Spirit as a member of the Trinity.

I looked around and saw a small group of people disappear into a rocky opening. I hastened in and caught up just as the guide was explaining that this was the "Apple Church," named so because of an apple tree that once grew nearby. It was also the largest of the seven churches in the Open Air Museum with four rock pillars supporting the central dome. Multi-coloured frescos spread across the walls and roof of the rocky interior narrating scenes from the life of Christ, the early saints, bishops, and martyrs. I looked up to see the face of Jesus painted within the dome.

Most of the fresco in the rock churches dated back to the Byzantine era between the 9th and 11th centuries. They had survived the course of history but like the martyrs, not without punishment. All the faces were badly disfigured and all the eyes had been chipped out. The guide was quick to defend the damage and told us that time and weather had eroded parts of the frescos. Time certainly has two hands, but it wasn't the hands of a clock that vandalized the frescos. Local religious tradition view painted and carved figures as symbols of idolatry, and they are especially wary of eyes. The eyes are the portal of the soul; one malicious look from an unbefriending person could transfer negativity and misfortune upon you. The markets in Göreme were full of amulets and talismans to combat this. One such talisman was "the evil eye," a small round blue object with white and blue concentric circles and a black spot in the centre. This served to catch the onlooker's attention and draw out any negativity before they focused on you.

I eavesdropped on another guide who seemed to be doing his best to confuse his group.

"And this one here," he said, pointing to a scene from the Last Supper, "is from the Old Testament. You can tell because there is only bread on the table and no fish."

I decided I would do the tour on my own and slipped away from the groups. I walked across to the six-story rock cliff that I had noticed when I first entered and stepped into a large, empty chamber on the first floor. A long stone table with stone benches occupied most of the chamber that once served as a dining hall and kitchen. I tried to imagine monks having a warm hearty meal on the cold, damp stone. There were small cave rooms to the left with oblong holes dug into the walls. These, I later learned, were beds. A large round millstone stood against one wall that was once rolled across the entrance to seal off the cave in the severe winter nights, or, whenever danger threatened. That would leave the occupants in a cold dark cell, sitting on stone-cold benches and sleeping in stone-cold beds.

The second level housed another ruined chapel, and to reach the church on the third, I had to pass through one of the many tunnels that connected each level. Imagining people living in these conditions was all too oppressive—I needed to get out into the sunshine. I decided to stick to the smaller churches on ground level.

"The Snake Church." I heard a guide call out as he led his group into the cave. I listened at the doorway, and when they came out, I went in. This was a burial chapel. The frescos were of a later period showing St. George killing the dragon, hence the name, "Snake Church," There were other frescoes of Constantine and his mother, Helena, holding a cross. Once again, the paint was chipped and gouged, not just on the faces, but also all over the images. I chatted to another guide on my way out, and he told me that there was a cave church on the far side that did not have much damage to it, but there would be another admission fee.

The Dark Church, so called, as it's only source of sunlight is a small window, was hidden in the clefts of rock near the monastery. It went undiscovered for centuries. The lack of sunlight preserved the beautiful red and blue hues of the painted walls. The frescos covered two chambers portraying the whole Gospel story as the monks would have taught it to their students and new converts. One wall alone relayed the life of Christ from His birth, to His baptism and transformation, all beautifully preserved.

My time was up. The museum was closing and I had to leave. There were still more churches to explore; a hundred and fifty in the whole Cappadocia region, but I was content with the few I had been privileged to see. Göreme left a deep impression on me of the difficult life the early Cappadocian believers endured. It is to these early Cappadocian Fathers and followers that we owe a debt of gratitude. Through their stalwart faith and perseverance, they laboured to define and preserve the doctrines of the faith that contributed to the stability of the early Orthodox Church and deeper understanding we have of the Scriptures today.

Underground Cities

The next morning I was up in time for a hearty Mediterranean breakfast and then off to catch the coach. I didn't have to wait long, and was soon climbing back out of the valley in the direction of Derinkuyu, one of the many underground cities of Cappadocia. Our guide, Alara, informed us that she had earned a degree in tourism with a major in Greek and Turkish history. I was all ears as she educated us on the area.

She proceeded with a lesson on Erciyes, the mother volcano that transformed the whole region into fairy chimneys and provided homes for thousands of desert dwellers. Erciyes was now in front of us and Alara talked about the volcano as if it were an old friend. Then the bus turned off the main road and slowly the venerated volcano disappeared out of sight behind us. Alara went on to tell us about the underground cities.

Below us, lay a multi-level, complex network of chambers and tunnels that made up 300 cities in total and spanned an area of 200 km in the region of Cappadocia. According to our knowledgeable guide, these cities were first dug out by the Hittites during the Median Empire, 10th - 7th century B.C. No one knows much about the Hittites, except for what is mentioned about them in the Bible. It is clear that the Christians had inhabited these subterranean communities as there is evidence of churches with baptism fonts. When Alara felt she had fed us enough information, she asked for feedback.

"Now who can tell me what they have learned today?" No one answered. I was sitting at the back, so I raised my hand and summarize as much as I could remember.

"Oh, you *are* listening," she said delightedly, and then sat down pleased that she had done her job.

We stopped halfway at a viewpoint where we all got off the bus to stretch our legs. I looked out over the hundreds of rock-pillar villages.

> He has made from one blood every nation of men to dwell on all the face of the earth, and has determined their pre-appointed times and the boundaries of their dwellings. — Acts 17:26

I pondered on the Scripture for a while. He made all mankind from one man, Adam. We are all as clay in the potter's hands. [17]

China, once again, filtered into my thoughts and I wondered how long I would go for. What did it matter, if that was where the Potter wanted me to live? Who was I, the clay, to object?

Our final stop at Derinkuyu drew a band of vendors, waving handmade Cappadocia dolls. One of the dear ladies singled me out to be the next adoptive parent to one of her dolls and followed me around, haggling relentlessly over the price. I had no idea how long we would wait before we went underground as Alara appeared to be in an altercation over the cost of the entrance tickets. Haggling seemed to be the way trade was conducted in the desert and the more noise one made the more they enjoyed it. I gave in and handed the vendor a few coins for the doll. Finally, Alara emerged with a victorious smile, waving our tickets at us as though to indicate that this was how it was done. I looked around for a natural cave entrance, but all I saw was a cement booth with an iron-gate. Alara ushered us in. I wasn't too happy about the thought of being locked in underground, but Alara assured us that the gate stayed open until everyone was out.

The passages were low, narrow, and sloping, but soon opened up into larger chambers. Eight levels of living spaces were organized around ventilation shafts that rose in different

6 Land of Beautiful Horses

conical shapes through the rock ceilings. Refectories, storage rooms, cellars, and even stables to tether small animals stood dark and empty, attesting to the once concealed lives of a languishing community.

Short natural passages connected the lower and upper floors, but the much longer ones were dug out by the ancients to link with other cities.

I peered down one more than a mile long and about a meter high. Any adult journeying through it would have had to walk bent over all the way.

Hewn pillars secured the larger chambers that were used as meeting halls and churches. We stepped into one complete with altar, stone benches, and a baptism font that was deep and wide enough to comfortably stand four people.

"How did they get so much water down here?" I ask Alara, after all this was below a desert. Alara shook her head. She had no idea. I looked around for evidence of subterranean wells, but all the holes were dry.

Alara motioned us towards the benches. We were about to experience a first century underground classroom. I wished I had brought something warm and soft to sit on.

"The disciples were schooled here," she said rather assertively. "In fact, the Apostle Paul taught in this very cave."

The New Testament does not mention the Apostle visiting the underground cities. However, after his conversion, Paul did return to Tarsus of Cilicia, his birthplace.[18] How long he stayed in Tarsus is unknown, but it's possible that it was several years. Cappadocia is about 240 km from Tarsus—quite a few days journey by foot.

Alara explained a little of the living conditions that hid over 30,000 people from their enemies; however, the caves were clearly not fit for human habitation. A toxic mineral within the limestone walls, calcitic limestone, or quicklime (CaO),[19] caused chronic lung conditions. Three weeks was all most people could endure.

After our lesson, I was able to explore a bit on my own. The dark tunnels were treacherous, and many lost their lives falling into pits or standing under ventilation shafts when their assailants threw down arrows and poured hot oil on them.

I tried to imagine living in these conditions with small children. They were not cavemen that hid from their oppressors, they were skilled and educated people who were forced to live like rats in the desert, escaping underground to survive attacks and then retreating to the volcanic rocks where they all eventually died for their faith. Everywhere I looked, the Psalms spoke to me:

> *Trust in Him at all times, you people; pour out your heart before Him: God is a refuge for us.* — Psalm 62:8

I looked down on a gridded pit:

> *You, who have shown me great and severe troubles, shall revive me again, and bring me up again from the depths of the earth.* — Psalm 71:20

I stopped at the baptism font:

> *Truth shall spring out of the earth, and righteousness shall look down from Heaven.* — Psalms 85:11

I bent down into the dark tunnels:

> *Out of the depths have I cried to You, O Lord; Lord, hear my voice! Let Your ears be attentive to the voice of my supplications.* — Psalm 130:1-2

My heart was pounding; I had to see the sun. The contrast of the sufferings of the early believers in comparison to the freedom of the western church of the twenty-first century seemed so brutally unfair. I consoled myself imagining them now rejoicing in heaven, rewarded for patiently enduring their trials, and wearing a martyr's crown.

Once everyone had emerged, we boarded the coach and drove on in silence towards Ihlara Village—this had to be more pleasant.

Canyon Chapels

The landscape was flat for miles around, except for a vertical 90-meter drop into the canyon below.

I stood peering over the rail, tracing the Melendiz River that forged this 16 km gorge, wondering if our guide was planning to take us down, and how long it would take if she did.

"We're going down," she said, as though she had heard my thoughts, "Just as soon as everyone is back together." Then she beckoned us to follow her as she descended the 400 steep steps.

Rocky walls and dark looming peaks closed in on us as we neared the canyon floor. The gorge was silent, as though resting from its turbulent past. Besides an eagle soaring above us, all was still. If the stones could cry out, what would they tell us? And then they did. We walked for about 10 minutes before Alara stopped and pointed to a cleft in the rocks.

"Another church!" she exclaimed and clambered over the large boulders towards it. We entered the little cave chapel with hewn pillars, arches, and domes in traditional church style, but the frescos here were from an earlier period, portraying the Gospel story in Arabian fashion with a very different style and colour to those in the Open Air Museum.

I looked up to the dome to see a picture of Jesus ascending into heaven with twenty-four angels surrounding Him. I stepped out again, thinking that was the only one.

"Oh, no," Alara explained, "there are over a hundred." A hundred churches and monasteries carved into the gorge, and all depicting the Gospel in pictures painted by Arabian, Egyptian, and Syrian Christians—what a story, what a Saviour!

Above the church I noticed rows of little dugout holes and asked Alara about them.

"They were homes for pigeons," she said. The birds flew across the valley carrying messages and also warnings of danger when enemies were approaching.

The Gospel had travelled like a flood from Jerusalem on the day of Pentecost and persecution followed right behind. The Anatolian desert offered refuge in the many tuffs and underground dwellings, and when there weren't enough places to hide, they carved out more in the gorge.

After a long arduous trek through the canyon, over boulders and sloping, stony contours, we finally came to a rest-camp alongside the river, where we were served lunch in true Turkish style. I sat down on a big square cushion and watched the flow of the Melendiz, while I dined on Turkish bread and lentil soup. I was done for the day, and ready to return to Göreme to some lighter evening entertainment; however, the day wasn't done with me just yet.

Get off the Bus

After our short respite, our coach wound its way to the end of Ihlara Valley and stopped at the foot of a huge cliff. I strained to see what the fuss was about ... a Cathedral on the top of a cliff? No, this time I was staying put, the hike through the valley had depleted me ... I soon found myself alone on the bus.

Cathedral? I thought, peering up at the enormous rock edifice. "Selime Monastery," the largest in all of Cappadocia, and carved into the cone of a dormant volcano. It must be amazing.

6 Land of Beautiful Horses

"Well, there's only one way to find out." I said to myself, and then pushing fatigue aside, I got off the bus and proceeded to scale the narrow winding path. From near the top of the cliff I could see the meandering Silk Road as it stretched through the village and across the hills as far as the horizon. Then over the hills and through village I traced the road back again, imagining the caravans of camels and traders making their way to this rock fortress where they found respite and protection from Arabian marauders.

The others in the tour group were quietly wondering in and out of the rock cubicles that once served as dwelling places for the ascetic monks. Behind me stood the intricately hewn two-story Monastery—I turned to look up at it. Darkness and gloom weighed down on me as I entered. I was too tired to take it in, and turned around to leave—after all, the beauty of the landscape was more appealing. I hesitated at the doorway. There was something in the walls—outlines of hidden figures beckoning me from behind a black veil. Another 13th century Gospel story, trapped in the modern, dark-age of unbelief? A closer look confirmed it ... beautifully painted frescoes enshrouded by the soot of the cooking fires from the Turkish occupation. And then, it was as though the cathedral was calling me back inside. The precision engineering and elaborate masonry of the stone pillars and arched windows whispered to me of the faith the monks displayed as they kneeled to pray. I noticed the detailed artwork around the altar and vestry portraying their love and dedication to the call. The volcano had kept it all alive, that we should not forget them. They must have been tired too, making the journey through the desert by foot and then climbing up the steep slopes of the volcano in the heat of the day.

I stepped outside into a small courtyard, imagining their gentle voices as they quietly tethered their mules at the rocky stable. The kitchen and living quarters testified to their lives and service. They had certainly left their mark for the modern world to see. Throughout the ages and despite the dangers, the Gospel went out from this evangelical outpost near the summit of a dormant volcano. And I would never have known if I hadn't got off the bus.

Only Islam Allowed

The next morning, after breakfast, I peered around the kitchen door and chatted with a Canadian lady busy at work. I asked her how she came to be at the pension and she told me her story.

She had met a Turkish man on business in Canada, and after a very brief courtship, they were married and then returned to settle in Turkey. The marriage didn't work out, and her husband went back Canada, leaving her penniless in Turkey. Having no family to call on, she proceeded to seek out employment. In a country were women are suppressed and many are forced to remain at home, this was not an easy task, and to complicate matters, she was diagnosed with cancer and had to have an operation to remove the tumour. Months after she recovered from her ordeal, the only work she could find was as a cook at a pension. At the time we spoke, she was still saving to pay her airfare back home.

I gasped at her situation and shared how Jesus had helped me through my difficulties, hoping she would allow me to pray with her. She said she would like prayer, but it was too dangerous.

"Only Islam is allowed here," she whispered. She knew of local Muslims who converted to Christianity and thereafter disappeared—they were never heard of again. I told her I would pray for her privately and asked if she would consider placing her trust in Jesus to help her to return home.

At that point, the manager came into the kitchen and militated against our peaceful conversation, bringing it to an abrupt end. He picked up pots and pans and dropped them down on the table making as much noise as possible. My Canadian friend jumped back to work and motioned for me to leave. I quickly collected my belongings and decided it was best to wait down in the village for the bus back to Nevşehir.

I sat down on a bench and quietly prayed that she would be protected from any punishment for discussing Christianity. Even the tour guides refuse to discuss Christian topics once the tours were over.

In Cappadocia alone, an untold number of Christians were martyred for hundreds of years from the inception of the early church with a short respite in the 9th and 10th centuries when all the rock churches were built.

The enemy hates this land, and no wonder, almost two thirds of the New Testament Epistles were written in it: Galatians, Ephesians, and Colossians. The Epistles of John and Peter were addressed to churches in Anatolia, and the seven churches of the Apocalypse in the first three chapters of Revelation were all in Anatolia.

The Ottoman Village

It was late when I arrived back at the apartment in Ankara. Bernard was waiting up for me.

"There's a job going in China you may be interested in," he said. "They're looking for someone to teach English at a business college."

"I'll never get a job at a university," I replied. "I don't have any experience."

"It's worth a try," he said encouragingly. I agreed to apply in the morning.

The rest of that week, I pondered on my bitter, sweet experience in Cappadocia, and the sadness I felt for believers who continue to be persecuted for their faith. I wished I could talk to the woman at the pension, to see that she was safe. She had told me how the manager had been pressing her to convert to Islam.

"I'm thinking of going to Beypazari this Saturday," Bernard said one evening. "It's an old Ottoman village. They have a lot of markets, very different to the ones we see downtown. And you can see how the other half lived," as though that was going to cheer me up!

Come Saturday morning, we caught two buses to Beypazari. The markets *were* different, there were traditional Turkish wares and trinkets, and we did enjoy exploring them. The village had a watering well in the centre for the animals. I was amused to see a donkey tethered in a parking space at the end of a row of parked cars. The grand old Ottoman houses were now hotels and pensions. What a stark contrast to the rock homes and churches of the persecuted Christians.

Passport to Fellowship

"I'd really like to go to church tomorrow," I said once we arrived home. "It's Easter Sunday."

"Okay," he replied, "but, it's a long way across town, and you'll need to bring your passport."

"My *Passport*? Why do I need my passport?"

"You'll see," he replied, and went off to bed. We were both tired from the long day.

The next morning we were up early for another tedious journey. We caught the campus bus into town and a second bus across town, and after that, a very long walk. We turned onto a street with stately looking buildings and high walls. Flags of various countries flew above each one.

"Are these embassies?" I asked him. We stopped outside the one flying the British flag.

Bernard turned to me and said, "Yes, this is where you need your passport. It's the British Embassy. I feel safer going to church here, on British soil."

We handed in our passports and walked up to a little chapel, already filling with foreigners and a few brave Turks who had come for the morning worship. It was a warm and jovial atmosphere where believers were free to talk about their faith.

Two weeks had passed by quickly. To my amazement, I had been offered the job in China and I needed to gather my thoughts and plan my next move. The visa application had to be submitted from my home country, South Africa.

Thankfully, my eldest daughter and family were still there, although their immigration papers were complete and travel tickets booked. They were due to leave South Africa four days after I was contracted to commence work in China. The timing was just perfect!

I looked online for the best flight deal. Within days, I was saying goodbye to my brother, not knowing when or where we would meet again, and I boarded a bus to Ankara airport.

Almost Cancelled from Above

It was a short flight to Istanbul, but we hit heavy turbulence over the infamous Bosphorus Strip; the worst I had ever experienced, and hope never to experience again. Overhead lockers dropped open, bags fell out everywhere, people were throwing up and oxygen masks were falling down. Needless to say, everyone was in a bit of a panic. I looked out the window to see the sea rising up to meet us and quickly assumed the brace position.

To take my mind off of my own fears, I proceeded to pray for the unsaved on board. I might have been the only Christian on the airplane.

With my head on my knees, and expecting to hit the water at any minute, I suddenly felt a sharp jolt, then the sound of grinding wheels. We were on the runway?

I sat up. Everyone cheered. For a minute there, I thought that my trip to China had been cancelled from above.

Temple of Heaven

7
God of China

See then that you walk circumspectly, not as fools but as wise, redeeming the time, because the days are evil.

Ephesians 5:15-16

CHINA HAS A 4,500 YEAR history with dynasties before the time of Christ, faithfully worshipping the God of the Old Testament as "Shang Di" 上帝 (Supreme God). The earliest records of worship can be found in the Shu Jing (Book of Historical Documents) where the Emperor Shun, in the year 2,230 B.C., offered animal sacrifices to Shang Di.

A modern researcher, Chan Kei Thong has documented evidence on his findings of Shang Di in his book, *Finding God in Ancient China*, published by Zondervan. His research shows the God of ancient China to be one and the same as the God of the Hebrews and the Christians.

Most of the chronicles recording China's history were compiled by the Chinese philosopher and sage, Confucius (551- 479 B.C.), in his Five-Volume Classics. These Classics were regarded as legendary and not historically correct until the discovery of the 'oracle bones' in 1899. (The bones revealed

WHEN ALL DOORS CLOSE

the names of emperors that once ruled China.) In more recent years modern archaeologist and researchers have confirmed the accuracy of Chinese recorded history with sufficient evidence to prove that the earliest Chinese dynasties not only existed, but they were highly skilled people and advanced for their time. [20]

Genesis in the Chinese Characters

The Chinese writing itself gives evidence to the knowledge the ancient Chinese had of God and the fall of man into sin. Numerous characters attest to the stories outlined in the book of Genesis. To list a few examples:

The word **forbidden**, 禁, is made up of 3 characters:

2 trees 木木 + a divine command 示 = 禁 [21] (Genesis 2:16-17).

The word **greed** (covet / desire), is made up of 2 trees 木木 + woman 女 = 婪 [22]

The word **fruit** is made up of 2 characters: tree 木 + garden 園 = 果

The word **naked** 衣果 [23] is made up of fruit 果 (tree + garden)+ clothing 衣 = 衣果

What has fruit, tree, and garden got to do with being naked, unless there is a story behind it? (Genesis 3).

The word **boat** 船 has 3 elements: vessel 舟 + 8 八 + mouth 口.[24]

Eight mouths / souls in a vessel = boat 船

> *On the very same day Noah and Noah's sons, Shem, Ham, and Japheth, and Noah's wife and the three wives of his sons with them, entered the ark.* — Genesis 7:13

How did this come about?

The Chinese believe that it all started at the Tower of Babel when God separated the people by mixing up their languages.

7 God of China

A group of worshipers who knew the events that followed the fall of Adam into sin and God's required sacrifice for worship, moved far north to the land of Sinim,[25] now called China. They wrote the story of creation and The Fall into the characters that made up their initial language.

Border Sacrifices

The emperors of the early dynasties continued to worship Shang Di, offering annual Border Sacrifices very similar to the order of sacrifice given to Moses. [26]

The sacrifices were first offered on a mountain on the border of Shandong province, and then later in the city at the site of the Temple of Heaven; originally called The Altar of Heaven, as God does not dwell in temples made by man. Over time, the pure worship of Shang Di became corrupted. [27]

Dragon King

Qin Shi Huang reunited China in 221 B.C. after the country had been divided for four centuries. Qin Shi Huang then became the first emperor of consolidated China from 221-206 B.C. He replaced the worship of Shang Di with the worship of "Dragon." He built the Great Wall,[28] parts of which are still standing today, although, to the Chinese, the Wall was never "Great," it was simply 10,000 Li-Long Wall.[29]

Among Qin Shi Huang's exploits were networks of highways, 500 miles longer than the Roman highways built two centuries later. His obsession with power led him to construct a mammoth underground tomb-city with an army of life-size terra-cotta warriors, where he could continue his reign in the afterlife. He called himself "The Dragon King" and showed no mercy to those who disagreed with him.

Qin Shi Huang is still known as the Ancestral Dragon. Many Chinese still refer to themselves as descendants of Dragon, and to their culture, as Dragon Culture. For nearly two millennia, the emperors that followed used Dragon Power to rule their subjects.

The Border Sacrifices were revived at the beginning of the Ming Dynasty in 1368 A.D., and continued with many of the emperors that followed until 1911 A.D. when China became a republic.

Although Shang Di was usurped by the Dragon King in 221-206 B.C., the Spirit of the Lord continued in the land. In Genesis chapter 3, God told the serpent (dragon) that he would bite the heel of man, but man would bruise his head. On my visit to, Shanhaiguan, I stood on Dragon's Head, the end of the Great Wall, where the Wall meets the sea. And, there I was able to proclaim, "Greater is He that is in me, than he that is in the world" (1 John 4:4 paraphrased).

The Missionaries

The most widely accepted record of the earliest Christians in China was found on a stone stele in 1623 A.D. dating back to 781 A.D. This stele records the journey of the Nestorian Christians who travelled from Syria on the Silk Road to Xian in 635 A.D.

However, in a more recent discovery, in 2002, a Chinese theological professor visited the "Han Dynasty Stone Relief Museum" in Jiangsu Province where he found numerous tombstones depicting the Nativity and the story of creation. [30] The tombstones had been excavated in 1995 from the tombs of aristocrats that dated back to the Han Dynasty, which ran parallel to the Roman Empire, 206 B.C. – 220 A.D.

In 2008, a French researcher, Pierre Perrier, was taken by a pastor of the underground church to the Kong Wang Cliff at the edge of Lianyungang, an area of the Silk Road. Here, he was shown Christian petroglyphs, previously discovered in 1980. The petroglyphs show the infant Jesus on the lap of His mother, engravings of the Eucharist, and the early disciples. Chinese scientists have dated the rock carvings to 65 A.D., confirming that Christianity came to China in the first century. [31]

Tolerance of Christianity in China waxed and waned throughout the centuries. The Franciscan monks arrived in the 13th century, and after their expulsion, the Jesuit monks in the 16th century. The Protestants arrived at the dawn of the 19th century with Hudson Taylor who founded the China Inland Missions, and by 1895, missionary outposts were established in every Chinese Province.

The People's Republic

In 1911, Sun Yat-sen brought an end to the imperial dynasties and became China's first provincial leader. Both Sun Yat-sen and Chiang Kai-shek, the first president of the Republic of China (1928-1949), were confessing Christians. It was only in 1949, when the People's Republic of China ushered in a socialist regime with an intolerance of all religions that the Church was once again suppressed and believers were forced to meet in secret.

I knew very little of the underground church before I went to China, and I only know little of it now. That's because the believers tread very carefully to protect the work of the Gospel. There is no need to know more than what you are involved in. Then you are not in any danger of exposing the efforts of others. Few books have been written on contemporary missions in China for this very reason.

We do know, through the underground pastors who are connected with a network of churches, that the body of believers is growing daily throughout the land, and mission outreaches continue to flow from China to other parts of Asia and North Africa. The Lord has always had "seven thousand" who have not bowed their knee to Baal. [32]

This is my story as I experienced the outworking of the Lord in my life in my short time there. For those I left behind, who still continue to faithfully promote the Gospel and win souls for the Kingdom of God, their names have been changed, fellowships cannot be mentioned, and locations will not be specified.

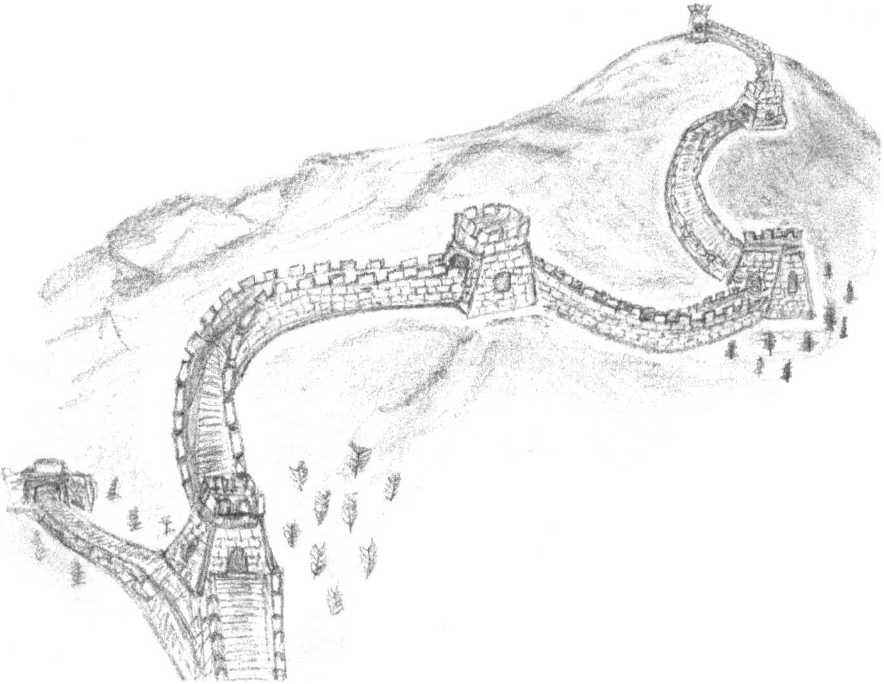

The Great Wall

8
Land of Dragon

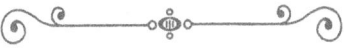

For we do not wrestle against flesh and blood, but against principalities, against powers, against the rulers of the darkness of this age ....

Ephesians 6:12a

I LANDED IN CHINA DURING THE H1N1 FLU epidemic. Cards were distributed on the airplane before we disembarked. We had to tick the boxes: headache ... no, sore throat ... no, blocked nose ... err, yes. I always have a bit of nasal congestion when I fly. I ticked the box and thought no more of it.

The minute I stepped off the flight-stairs and into the transit lounge, I was ushered into a makeshift medical booth and repeatedly asked a battery of questions.

"No," I answered over and over, "I'm not sick." Now that I was off the plane, I could breathe freely; my sinuses were clear. That didn't seem to satisfy the medical attendants; they continued with the interrogation, so I demonstrated to them.

"Look, I can breathe," I said, holding one finger against the left nostril and inhaling deeply and then I did the same with the right. Finally, I was given another form to fill in requesting my final destination with the full address and number of a contact person. Only then was I allowed to enter China.

Once through, I purchased a connecting ticket and a mobile phone and called my contact to let him know my estimated time of arrival. It was after midnight when I finally reached my destination, and I was relieved to see the foreign secretary waiting patiently. It's only on our first arrival that we get this kind of assistance, after that we have to find our own way. He appeared to be in a cheerful mood, despite the late hour and chatted to me about the college and the student intake.

"There are over 2,000 universities in China," he said, "and every year six million students graduate, but can't find jobs. Another six million register, and so the cycle continues." Then, after the usual talk about the weather, he could see I was tired from my gruelling flight and let me rest for the remaining journey to the university campus.

It was dark and deserted when we arrived. We stopped outside a building and I was told to wait inside while he went in search of a key.

"This is not going to be your permanent home," he said, on his return. "It's only for a short while." He led me up two flights of stairs and to a small dingy room on the third floor. In China, the first floor starts on ground level. "I'm very sorry," he continued, as he turned the key and indicated that I should enter. "But, you are placed in quarantine for three days." I didn't answer. I was too tired to care.

"There's a café across the street where you can get your meals, but please don't talk to any of the students." He handed me the key and before he turned to go, he told me to call him if I have a fever, and then he disappeared down the stairs. I dropped my things on the floor and then dropped myself on the bed and fell fast asleep.

8 Land of Dragon

I awoke to the sounds of gunshots, and in my half-sleep state, I thought I was back in South Africa where it was not uncommon to be disturbed in the night by gunfire. I sat up with a jolt: *This wasn't South Africa!* I quickly reached for the bedside light. It was 4 a.m. and still dark outside. Where were the shots coming from, and why? This was, after all, a university campus. It must be coming from the streets. There were three more shots, and then it stopped. I dosed off again and my next rude awakening was to shouting right outside my window.

"*Yi, er, san, si,*" (1,2,3,4) a voice called, and a throng of voices repeated, "*yi, er, san, si.*" I jumped up and peered out to see a small platoon of uniformed youths being marched down the street and round a corner. I started to question whether I was in the right place, or if the job I'd applied for was on a military college campus. That question was not going to be answered for the next three days as I was forbidden to speak to anyone.

I looked around the room taking stock in the morning light. There were two beds and a small chest of drawers. Papers were lying on the floor and the carpet looked like it hadn't been vacuumed for months. It was clearly a student dorm. I grabbed my toothbrush and checked the bathroom—only one tap working. The showerhead over the bath was missing and so was the washer. Water trickled out of the pipe and when turned on, it wasn't that much stronger. The bathtub was yellow with grime—definitely not going to sit in that. I decided I was clean enough for the next three days. Trying my best not to be intimidated by the gunshots and the bellowing and the dirty bathroom, I decided to get a breath of fresh air and go in search of breakfast.

It felt good to be out in the sunlight. I looked up at the building I had just exited. It looked rather grand, painted white with many different foreign flags flying across the entrance.

Students were coming and going from all the buildings including the café across the street. Many were still arriving with bags and books in hand. No one seemed to notice a foreigner until I stepped into the café.

It was fairly busy. Even though I tried not to make eye contact with anyone, I was clearly the centre of attention. This was a student's café, not a place where teachers frequented, so it was assumed that I was a new student. I walked down the rows of open food bowls, failing to identify any of them. Then I saw a woman cracking eggs, and I pointed to them, indicating that I would have two. I had no way of communicating how I wanted them cooked, so I stood back and watched as she dropped them onto a large hot plate, chopped up some black rubbery looking substance, and then scrambled them all together. When done, she scooped it all up into a bowl of rice and then looking up at me and pointed to a row of black jars containing a tar like substance with well-used paintbrushes. I quickly held my hand up and shook my head. I took the scrambled rice and the chopsticks she offered, paid her for the meal, and made for a seat in the far end of the café away from the students.

"Do you want friend?" I soft voice spoke behind me. I turned around to two big shiny, brown eyes and the broad smile of a young girl.

"Oh, that's okay," I tried not to sound impolite. "I can sit here on my own, thank you."

"No, I sit with you," she insisted, and then proceeded with her line of questioning.

"You first time here?"

"Yes, my first time here."

"You, want friend? I be your friend." Two more young girls joined us, intrigued by the new *laowai* (foreigner)

"Where you come?'

"South Africa,' I replied

"*Nǎn fēi,*" they all exclaimed. At least they spoke a little English, so I could make my next question clear.

"What's this?" I asked pointing to the black substance chopped up in my egg-rice.

"*Aah ...,*" they all expressed together and rattled off in Mandarin. They shook their heads.

"Is it a vegetable?" I tried to narrow it down.

"No, no vegetable."

"Well, is it meat?" I tried again.

"No, no meat."

I looked puzzled. "No, vegetable, no meat?" They nodded their heads in agreement.

"We don't know English word," said the first girl, and then assured me, "It's good, you eat." She nodded with a big smile. Whatever it was, it didn't have much taste, a bit salty. It turned out to be seaweed, but it took me a few weeks to pin that down. After breakfast, my little trio of friends walked me out of the café.

"You go to class now?" one of the girls asked.

"No, I'm not a student, I'm a teacher."

"*Lao shi,*" they said in surprise and took a step back.

"It's okay," I assured them, "I don't mind you talking to me."

"Teachers don't eat here," they said pointing to the café.

"I'm staying over there," I replied pointing to the big white building with the flags.

"Aah, we go now," they all said together. I made my way back to my solitary confinement.

The weekend passed quickly. Students kept coming and going in the building, doors kept slamming, soldiers marching, people shouting, and all while I was prepping for Monday's class. I found a small store near the café where I could get yogurt, bananas, and sweet bread rolls for my daily meals.

On Sunday evening, I was startled by a sharp knock on my door. I opened to see the foreign secretary clutching a clipboard.

"Hello, do you have a fever?"

"No, I'm fine."

"Good, you can start class tomorrow." He said and then proceeded to give me directions to the business college on the other side of the campus. If I cut through the campus square, I could make it in 15 minutes. My classroom was on the sixth floor and there were only two elevators in the building for 3,000 students and 100 teachers and staff. I would have to add another 10 minutes to make it up the stairs.

"There's a meeting for you at lunch-break on the 5th floor, please don't be late!"

My first trip across the campus square on Monday morning immersed me in waves of students hurrying in every direction. The soldiers marched down the middle of the road in regimental style and everything moved out of their way including the cars. It was clear that the military ruled. I reached the middle of the square and looked up at the national flag hoisted above a podium that was decorated with dragonheads. Up until that point, I had been singing to myself to muster confidence for the task ahead, but now I was stilled by a presence around the podium. There was something even more unsettling about the flag than the first night's gunshots and the military marching. I questioned myself as to why I should be so disturbed by a flag—it was not as if it could hurt me.

I reached the college and climbed the six flights of stairs, passing hundreds of students, some going up and others coming down. The ones coming down didn't step aside for anyone, including teachers; it was survival of the fittest to get to class. I soon learned why. Tardiness was penalized on a daily basis and the demerits reflected on their final paper. The college did not tolerate any misconduct of any kind or form. On the up side, I knew I wasn't going to have much trouble with the students, but this was still my first day, and I hadn't been informed of any of the rules yet. The fill-in was only at lunchtime.

I stepped into a classroom of about 40 students. Those who were not supposed to be there quickly fled and the rest quieted down as they took their seats. For the first time, I noticed how very tall some of the boys were, and their stalwart stares only added to my already unsettled nerves. Determined not to let my apprehensions betray me, I stepped up to each one and took their names and asked them where they were from and what their majors were. I had a register of names like Heaven, Spring, Rain, and Flower from the girls, and Watermelon, Apple, and Summer from the boys. Most students choose English names that sound similar to their Chinese names, meanings are not important.

Little did I know that they were just as wary of me as I was of them? I was something of an enigma. They had never seen a fair-skinned foreigner with such dark hair. They thought that only Chinese people had dark hair and the rest of the world was blond, brown, or amber. As it turned out I was the only one on staff with brown/black hair, and from behind, I could be mistaken as Chinese.

Once I started to share about myself and my country, the tension subsided and we talked about what they hoped to learn from their English classes. At 12 p.m. when class was over, I went in search of the boardroom. There were many foreign teachers from various countries, mostly from the USA. I introduced myself to those close by and then took a seat and waited for instructions. I was asked the usual questions of, where I was from and when I had arrived.

"Four days ago," I replied, "I've just come out of quarantine." And then every head turned in my direction.

"Quarantine?"

'Yes," I said, "I was told to stay in quarantine for three days. Wasn't everyone?"

"No," they replied, looking rather bewildered. "We've all been on a tour of the city. Why did you have to be quarantined?"

"I don't know, I thought it was standard procedure for everyone." At this point, they all burst out laughing.

"There must have been some mix up. Are you sure you weren't sick?"

"I'm sure." I replied, and turned to my notes to avoid any more embarrassing questions.

We were briefed on the rules and policies and it was made clear that speaking about religion, sex or politics to the students was strictly forbidden. We were informed that spies would be present in all our classes and they were to report all our activities and discussions. The spies were student leaders of the communist party and we soon came to know who they were.

After the meeting, I went straight to the foreign secretary for an explanation as to why I was the only one who had been quarantined.

"Those were my instructions," he said apologetically. "You were sick at the airport." So, the airport authorities had called the college and told them to lock me up! Dragon did not approve of my arrival. I decided to take it as a compliment.

Retaliation - The Tail of Dragon

My three days in the student dorm turned into three weeks before I was allocated an apartment, and yes, I did take an occasional shower in the grimy bathtub. On one of my morning walks across the campus square, singing a Gospel song to myself to muster confidence, I felt an uncomfortable presence again right under the flag, but this time much stronger. I had experienced this kind of atmospheric heaviness in South Africa when around the sangomas (witchdoctors), and in many of

England's old houses, and once when I happened upon a pagan wedding within a stone circle and drew near to observe. It was as though something had stepped across my path to challenge me. Instead of hurrying along, I reacted to the challenge and sassed it. The moment the words were out of my mouth, I knew I had made a big mistake—Dragon has a long tail of retaliation. I hurried along repenting of my stupidity and praying for wisdom and protection. I was, after all, on Dragon's territory, and should be more vigilant.

Although it seemed slow at the time, the three weeks did pass by quickly. I adjusted to my new tasks and got acquainted with the students. I would amuse them with my efforts to speak Mandarin and they would amuse me with their English pronunciation.

"Try some snake!" one of the girls said with a big grin as she held up a dark dried out strip for me to take.

"No, thanks," I replied. "I don't eat snake."

"But, my mother make it," she insisted. "It's good snake." I looked into her eager shiny eyes and knew that if I didn't take it, I was going to disappoint her, and we had only just begun a sure friendship.

"Okay, I'll try it later, I'll take it home." I took the long dark strip and on a closer look I saw that it was a piece of dehydrated brinjal (eggplant), a vegetable native to the Southern Asian continent and common in South Africa.

"Oh, you mean snack," I cried in relief. "I'll try it later."

"Yes, that's what I say, snake!" she affirmed, relieved that I finally got it right.

*****

The freshmen were still on their daily marches: up at 5 a.m. for an hour of physical exercises with a short recess for breakfast and then back to marching. At 11 a.m., they stood for 45 minutes in front of the main building without moving, except for those who fainted. I watched them from my office window and sneaked a few pictures with my digital camera. When they finally came to class after their gruelling three weeks training, they were tired and irritable. The girls especially, hated it. They were demoralized by the fact that they had to spend so much time in the sun. A fair complexion is held in high esteem in their culture; something every self-aware Chinese maiden diligently protects with a very large umbrella when out in the sun. Now, the girls faces were severely darken with sunburn. They felt miserable about themselves and saturated their skin with lightening creams.

"The sunburn will fade in a couple of weeks," I tried to reassure them, but the damage was done and they were inconsolable.

There was a long weekend coming up at the end of my first three weeks and my new apartment was ready. It didn't take long for me to move in, as I only had one suitcase and a few books, but I was in dire need of kitchen utensils. We were provided with the basic furniture: a bed, chairs and table, and a pot and pan in the kitchen, but no crockery or cutlery. Friday was a public holiday and there would be no classes; it was perfect timing for me to settle in. I caught the bus to the local store and shopped for the necessities.

It was late when I returned and the apartment building was quiet. Most of the teachers took advantage of the long weekend and went sightseeing. I busied myself with unpacking and unclipping my purchases. The plastic clips in China are much stronger than the ones I was used to back home in South Africa, and the knives are a whole lot sharper. I slid a small kitchen knife under the plastic to free one of the utensils, as I would have normally done back home.

8 Land of Dragon

The plastic strip was unyielding and the razor sharp knife slipped into the palm of my hand. The moment it pierced my flesh a bright red flag flashed across my face—Dragon had swung his tail. I pressed hard on the wound to stop the bleeding and then went knocking on all the doors on my level.

Everyone was out, so I called Sharon, one of my colleagues, who put me in touch with a local teacher who lived nearby. He informed me of a street clinic in walking distance from the main gate of the campus, but I would have to wait until morning, as he didn't think they were open after hours. I checked the wound—it needed stitching. I wasn't planning on taking a taxi to a hospital without an interpreter, so I bandaged it up tightly and went to bed.

The following morning I found the clinic, and as it turned out, it *was* open 24 hours. I was soon ushered into a booth and sat down on a stool while a nurse opened the now closing wound so she could clean it properly. After three stitches, an antibiotic and some painkillers, I was on my way. Shaken by the whole ordeal, I resolved to not speak or sing a word about my faith to anyone, or anything, for the rest of my stay. Once I had fulfilled my contract, I would be on my way and out of China. After waiting all these years to come, all I wanted now was to leave.

[I know that one cannot attribute every little mishap to the enemy. I experienced many other incidents in my three-year stay, and two of them were dangerous falls, but I was certain that the flag flashing before my eyes when I stabbed my hand was a demonic threat and not a careless accident.]

The Author with Simon

9
Teacher, Tell Me About God

The Lord will perfect that which concerns me.

Psalms 138:8a

SIMON WAS A STUDENT WITH a very inquiring mind and he was curious about God. At first, he seemed nervous as he stood around waiting for an opportunity to talk to me. He would stay behind after class and chat about the lesson and his plans for the future. He offered to serve as an interpreter when I needed help in the local markets. I had many offers from the students. They love to hang out with the foreign teachers and gain favour with them and at the same time improve their English. When Simon offered, I felt a nudge from within to accept, and so we arranged to meet the following Saturday to take a trip into the city.

The buses were always packed with students, especially on a Saturday morning; we barely had any standing room. The shoving, pushing, and shouting was all part of the experience that one had to get used to as the bus ride was an hour long. It was at that time that Simon decided to broach the subject he had been itching to talk to me about.

"Teacher, tell me about God." He said in his deep loud voice that he now raised an octane or two to be heard above the noise. I quickly looked around to see if anyone had heard him.

"No, not here," I replied.

"Why not?" He looked puzzled.

"I'm forbidden to talk about my faith to any of the locals, especially students. It's one of the rules. I could lose my job and be told to leave the country." I whispered back.

"Oh, okay." He replied softly, but as soon as we got off the bus, he looked at me intently.

"What do you want to know about God, Simon?" I said reluctantly, as I was still bent on not discussing my faith with anyone.

"I want to know how you tell God's love from loving others, you know, like when a boy loves a girl?" he asked in earnest.

"Oh, so you *do* believe in God," I replied.

"Yes, when I was nine years old my mother took me to a church, but only once. In the church I felt love inside me." He patted his chest as he spoke. "And, sometimes, when I sit and think about God, that love comes back, I feel warm inside." He patted his chest again.

"Yes, Simon, that's God's love. It's very peaceful and warm and you don't have to do anything to receive it. God gives His love freely and He has a wonderful plan for your life." I explained how God gave His Son, Jesus, to be sacrificed for ours sins, and He is our only means of salvation. Simon listened carefully, and nodded that he understood.

In the days that followed, I found myself repeatedly musing over Simon's question, and as I did, the Lord's love filled my heart too. Perfect love casts out all fear. [33] I knew I would not be able to remain silent for very long. I understood what David meant when he said:

9 Teacher, Tell Me About God

I was mute with silence, I held my peace even from good; and my sorrow was stirred up. My heart was hot within me; while I was musing, the fire burned. Then I spoke with my tongue.
— Psalm 39:2-3

Immersing into Culture

I had much to learn about the mores and beliefs of the locals. In one of my classes, we discussed popular proverbs and I quoted a few of Confucius'—those I was acquainted with from my school days. I thought it would help build rapport, but unknowingly, I had stepped out of line. One of my students, who called himself Achilles, approached me very discretely after class and very politely said:

"Teacher, you cannot discuss our philosophers until you have learned something about our language, history, and culture."

Now that was a challenge I could not ignore.

"Okay," I replied. "I will try to learn about your language, history, and culture, and then can we talk about it?"

Achilles had a contagious smile. His eyes brightened as he answered, "Yes, and I want to talk about *your* religion, I believe there's something in it too. Many people in China believe."

*****

Every college has its own policies, but all local employees have to be members of the communist party to hold a position on campus; however, this is not a requirement for foreign teachers, many of whom are Christians. So, I was very surprised, when one Friday afternoon, while working in the office, I looked up to see Chéng (not his real name), one of the Chinese teachers, enter with a familiar black book under his arm.

"Is that a Bible?" I asked surprised.

"Yes," he answered, quickly glancing down at it, as if to check that it was still there.

"What are you doing with a Bible?" I knew from previous conversations, that he was not a believer.

"I'm writing a paper on it," he replied, matter-of-factly. At that moment, a hundred questions raced through my mind. I took a deep breath and focused on one.

"What are you going to write on?" I stood up to take a closer look—it was indeed a "Bible."

"I'm not sure yet," came a nonchalant reply.

"Well, when do you have to have this paper done by?" I singled out another question.

"Monday," he answered, now standing at his desk still clutching the Bible under his arm as though it was super-glued to him. I wondered why he didn't put it down, and then I fell back in my chair at the thought of someone attempting to sum up the Bible with all its doctrines, historical accounts, poetry, songs, Gospels, and Epistles in the space of two days. My biggest, 100th question was, "WHY?"

A foreign teacher sitting right next to him, also a believer, jumped at the opportunity and pulled out a handful of Gospel tracts.

"Here, take these, it will help you with your paper," he said eagerly. At that point, an even bigger shock awaited me. Chéng, still holding the Bible under one arm, retracted from the tracts as though they would bite him.

"I can't take those. They're Christian!"

I ducked down behind the partition that separated my desk from the others. I didn't know whether to laugh or cry. Chéng had no regard for the Bible as a divinely written book! I looked up again.

"It's, okay Chéng, we're not trying to convert you." I explained to him that the Bible is very intense, and too profound

9 Teacher, Tell Me About God

to write a paper on in two days. He might find it easier to choose a topic and narrow it down to one or two points, and the tracts would merely aid him in finding a theme that he could focus on.

"Oh," he replied, "if it will help me write my paper, then maybe I'll take them." He reached out and accepted the tracts, and, of course, they were all on the Gospel of salvation. Still bursting with questions that I could not ask in that office, I quickly went in search of another of my colleagues.

Peter was a foreign teacher and a former pastor. He had been in China a long time and was well acquainted with college policies and culture. He explained that in some colleges in China, the Bible is used to teach English. It is regarded by many as a great literary work, just as we would view the works of Shakespeare; full of poetry, prose, history, and intrigue. Except for one thing, the Bible, to them, was a book of myths and legends. Chéng had been taking lessons in English using the Bible as an English set book. On the up side, in these places, it opened the way for others to use the Bible as an English tool too. Peter invited me to an off campus "English Corner" at his home that evening where I saw "poetry in motion" as a dozen, or so students listened to the Scriptures to improve their English.

Peter also invited me to accompany him on a faith walk around the campus. Once a week, he and a few others went in small groups of two or three, so as not to raise attention. Of course, I was eager to join in. He also filled me in on the religious policies of the "Three-Self Patriotic Movement."

The Three-Self Church was the title given to all the Chinese governed churches, where the three principles of: Self-governance, Self-support, and Self-propagation were upheld. The Three Self Rule dictates the following:

1) Self-governance - no foreigner may partake in leadership, or ministry.

2) Self-support – Chinese churches are to remain financially independent from foreign aid.
3) Self-propagation - missionary work is to be conducted by the indigenous people only. Foreign missions are not permitted in China.

I later learned that these three Principles were first drafted by the Church Missionary Society in 1841, and then formally drafted at a Shanghai conference in 1892. The principles were meant to encourage the local Chinese to take responsibility in establishing their own indigenous churches. It was in 1951 that the Three Principles were drafted into the "Patriotic Movement" in order to remove foreign influences altogether from the Chinese churches. This was to ensure patriotism of the churches to the People's Republic of China. It also allowed the government to infiltrate and control the churches.

There were other rules enforced on the pastors. Topics that are forbidden in their sermons: The Holy Spirit, the sovereignty of God, the gifts of the Spirit, the Second Coming, or anything on the Book of Revelation to name a few. All Sunday sermons are recorded and forwarded to the local police station.

No one under the age of 18 years is permitted to attend church. Students who want to go to church have to report their attendance to their group leaders, and they are not permitted to attend every week.

Foreigners can attend a Chinese service, but they are forbidden to take part in any way. In most places, foreigners have the freedom to worship together as they please; however, the locals are forbidden to attend the foreign fellowships.

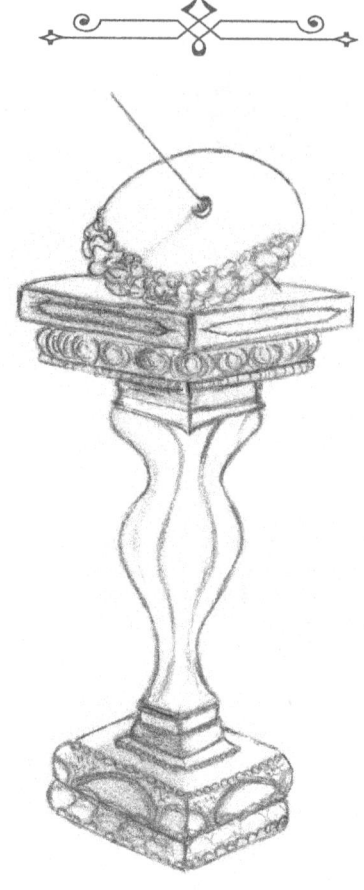

Sundial - Forbidden City

10
An Appointed Time

For the vision is yet for an appointed time; but at the end it will speak, and it will not lie.

Habakkuk 2:3

ON MY FIRST FAITH WALK, when we passed our college building, I felt an excitement stirring within me. I envisioned an outreach in the foyer of the building. I shared this with the group. Peter shook his head and said that it was not a good idea; permission would never be granted. If we tried anything like that, we risked arrest and a very heavy fine, or immediate deportation. He reminded me that this was still communist China; besides, the foyer was furnished with large armchairs that the soldiers used to loiter in at lunchtime when they were training on campus; there was hardly any room for an outreach. I dismissed the idea as naive zealousness. I was a new-comer and I still had a lot to learn about the struggles of those who had tarried there a long time.

We walked on, but the impression would not leave me. I felt a gentle assurance that the Lord would work in the hearts of the authorities to allow the outreach. Still, I thought it best not to press the issue and decided to say no more about it.

October 1st 2009 marked the 60th anniversary of the People's Republic of China. The streets were even more crowded than usual and there were protests in various places. We were advised to stay on campus. I remembered how the student protests of 1989 in Tiananmen Square ended and thought it best to follow instructions. There was now an increase in Christian persecution. We heard about the recent assaults made on house churches—it was definitely a time to exercise caution.

I focused on my classes. The challenges of compiling English lessons with no material and very little internet access were difficult enough. I sought advice from the other English teachers only to find that everyone worked independently with their own material. There was no uniform syllabus or lesson plan, and the college library didn't have much I could draw from either. I talked to my supervisor.

A Daunting Task

"Yes, we do want a uniform syllabus, but no one has the time, we're all too busy. It would have to be voluntary work; the college is not prepared to employ a course writer."

Oh, I thought, to myself; that is a huge task. I had worked on courses before in the ministry, but I wasn't an expert in English, or syllabi setting. All the same, I definitely needed assistance with my lesson planning. I enquired as to whether there was an academic bookshop in the city that might sell English books. I found a colleague who knew the exact location and was planning a trip there over the weekend for the same reason—to find material for lesson planning.

10 An Appointed Time

The next Saturday we caught the bus downtown and made our way to the top floor of a bookshop where all the English books were shelved. We went through all the academic books and singled out the most user-friendly and economical ones. After making satisfactory purchases, confident that they would be a great help, we returned to the campus.

Drawing out lesson plans from the material for my own personal use was fairly easy, but comfort zones are not the dwelling places of disciples—the Lord is always stretching us and growing us in His plans. I felt a prompting from within that I should write the syllabus. For a while I was at a loss as to where to start. When God calls, He also provides—help was not too far away.

One day, at lunchtime, while I was alone in the office and at my desk working through my new books, Neil, one of the English teachers, walked in.

"What are these?" he asked, picking up a book and flipping through it.

"User-friendly books," I replied.

"They look good," he said encouragingly. "I might get some too." I looked up at him.

"Know anything about English language syllabus writing?"

"A bit," he replied. "Why?" I relayed my conversation with the supervisor.

"I didn't know the college wanted a syllabus," Neil said. "I could help with that."

"You could?" I replied eagerly.

"Yes, as a matter of fact, I'm doing my Ph.D. in classification and reasoning, and this could be good practice for me."

"They're not going to pay any extra for it, and the other teachers may not be interested in using it," I added.

"That's okay, as I said it would be good practice for me, and I would use it, too." He pulled up a chair and immediately proceeded to draw up an outline for the first task. In the weeks that followed, he acquired a full set of books and drew up an outline on the language functions of each chapter. I worked to fill in the objectives and suggestions for oral exercises. He checked all my work and advised me along the way. Then we put them to the acid test—in the learning centres.

The students perked up. The lessons and activities were stimulating and enforced learning. The supervisors got to hear about it, and very soon the books were in every classroom and all the teachers were working from a uniform syllabus. And, the Lord was working out His plan for me.

I continued in the weekly faith walks, and each time we passed by our college building I would experience the same inner excitement at the thought of an outreach in the foyer. I felt we were to hold it at Christmas time. Still, I kept it to myself. Whatever the Lord wills to do, He will do, His way, and in His time.

Old Beijing Town

11
He Calls His Own

My sheep hear My voice, and I know them, and they follow Me.

John 10:27

SHARON WAS FROM TEXAS, BUT she had lived in China some time and spoke fluent Mandarin. She introduced me to some of the home fellowships and took me to visit one of the earlier protestant churches, established in the 19th century; now under control of the 3 Self-Patriotic Movement.

We arrived late and the church was full, but we were kindly ushered to the front row where seats had been reserved for visitors. The order of service was conducted in the same manner as an English Protestant service, complete with a choir dressed in long black gowns. The only difference was that the hymns and message were in Chinese, not English.

After the service, Sharon led me around the back of the church where we entered another three-story building. On every level, there were large rooms with wooden pews to accommodate those who could not find a seat in the main hall.

Here, they could sit and listen to the same service via telecast. This was evidence of how hungry people were for the Word of God once the religious tolerance ban had been lifted. Those who wanted to experience the baptism of the Holy Spirit would have to seek the underground church pastors as this was forbidden. I was curious to know how one finds the underground pastors.

The following weekend, while we were at a downtown restaurant discussing how we could share the Gospel on the streets without landing in trouble, two local ladies approached us. They didn't speak English so Sharon spoke to them in Mandarin, while I prayed that she could share the Good News. They asked us who we were and where we were from, but they were even more curious to know whether we were Christians. They were believers and wanted to know if we were too. They were keen to talk about their faith, something they could never do in public, and especially not with foreigners. I believe that the Holy Spirit led them straight to us. *That's how they find the underground pastors,* I thought. *They are led by the Holy Spirit.* And my thoughts were soon confirmed.

One afternoon there was a knock on my door. The landlady told me that a student requested a visit and asked if I would receive her. There were rules regarding student visits in the teacher's apartment; visitors had to be cleared with security and permission obtained from the teacher first. They were not permitted to stay more than two hours.

Not long after, I heard a gentle knock, and I turned to see a young freshman girl shyly waiting for permission to enter. Her English was weak and she struggled to explain herself, but she wanted to share her testimony. I encouraged her to take her time and I would try to follow. She had not been a believer until high school, when she had had a dream about Jesu (Jesus). She told me that Jesu spoke to her and said, "I am coming soon!"

11 He Calls His Own

I asked her if anyone had shared the Gospel with her before. She shook her head. I asked her how she knew about Jesus. No one had told her about Jesus before, and yet, she knew when she saw Him in her dream that His name was Jesu.

She had heard that one of her former schoolteachers was a Christian, so she shared her dream with him, and then he told her how to be saved. He too, had dreams about Jesus that he shared with her, but she was not allowed to repeat them. I asked her if any others had dreams like this. She nodded and smiled. I told her how happy I was to hear her testimony then we prayed together before she left. She changed her English name to remind her of her dream, as she now lives in hope that Jesus will return for her too.

On another occasion, a pastor from one of the underground churches came to visit with his wife and daughter. They shared their struggles as believers and how the network of underground churches functioned in spite of all the difficulties.

"The underground churches are everywhere," he said, "We don't meet in the same place every week and we can't advertise where the next meeting will be, but everyone always turns up." He laughed. "The Holy Spirit tells them where to go. This confuses the spies. They can never find us."

Foreigners were not encouraged to attend these meetings as it raised suspicion. I shall never forget his daughter's face; it glowed as though the sun was shining on her. The young Eastern believers portray a passion for Jesus that is rarely seen in the youth of the Western cultures.

I had been told to wear a cross at college to make it easier for the believing students to identify me; however, when talking to one of my students, he said it wasn't necessary.

"It's easy to know who the Christian teachers are; they're always happy and smiling." Still, I wanted to connect with the

Christian students, so I wore a cross to class; I could identify *them* by their approving smiles. Not much was said in class because of the spies, but I soon came to know my spiritual family on campus.

So Much to Learn About God?

One day as I was walking along to class chatting to one of my students, he turned to ask me what I had studied to earn a degree.

"Theology," I replied. His eyes widened.

"What's that about?" He asked. When I told him, it was the study of the nature and character of God and all of God's great works, his eyes widened even more.

"There is so much to learn about God?" he exclaimed.

"Yes, there is, and so much more. Ten degrees wouldn't be enough." And then I told him how equally surprised I was to find out that the university offered three different Masters Degrees in Marxism. I didn't think there was so much to learn about an ideology either.

"Do you want to know what the best thing was, that I learned in theology?" I asked, jumping at the opportunity to share some Good News without any spies in earshot. He looked up at me and smiled without answering, he knew I was going to tell him whether he wanted to hear it, or not.

"Well, it's that God is love and He loves you, and He has a wonderful plan for your life."

12
No Monkeys in Heaven

The fool has said in his heart, "There is no God."
Psalm 14:1

CHRISTMAS CAME AND WENT AS we worked through the holidays. The foreign teachers were given Christmas Day off, but come the 26th, it was back to class. As the cold winter set in, I prepared to leave for the long semester break. The week before my departure, I went down to the admin-office to obtain a letter giving me permission to exit the country for my break. I needed the letter to apply for an Australian visa.

The administrator approached me and asked if I would take a cultural anthropology class as a TA (teacher assistant) in the next semester. Some of the graduate students were taking anthropology as an elective to raise their marks for a postgraduate course. If the class is very small they won't pay a foreign lecturer to fly out, instead, they get one of the teachers on campus to teach from the lecturer's notes and confer with the lecturer before and after class. I couldn't accept. I had no experience in anthropology to answer questions and I knew it would require an enormous amount of time and energy just to get acquainted with the subject. I still had to cover my English classes as well. Besides, I was trained in theology and adhere to the belief that "In the beginning, God created ..." I firmly oppose the precepts and suppositions of evolution. I believe that evolution still has a stronghold over the world because God is a gentleman, and He does not force His ways on anyone. I side with William of Wykeham of the 14th century, who said, "Manners maketh man," *not* "monkey maketh man."

The next day I received a phone call from the administrator.

"You're the best person to do this. We don't have anyone else, and you'll get an increase." She tried to sound persuasive. "Please think about." I said I would, and I later mentioned it to Sharon in the office.

"It would be a challenge," she said. "And what better person than a theology major. Think of the opportunity to give your point of view, no one else here would be allowed to do that."

Sharon was right! It might be a great opportunity to talk about creation and the message of salvation. I prayed about it for a couple of days, and then felt I should accept the challenge, but there was one condition. I would only take the class if I could present an alternate view on creation, which I proposed as: "Intelligent Design." That, of course, stirred a hornet's nest in the main office, but I stood my ground. For a moment, I thought the Dean was going to be summoned, and I was going to get my marching orders. Instead, they said they would contact the lecturer, who was in the USA, to see if my terms would be acceptable. They obviously had no one else to take the class; I was given permission to present my views. However, it was made clear that I had to cover the chapters on evolution, as the exam was set from the textbook. I was told I would be sent all the material to my Australian address. I left for my long vacation, and when the material arrived, it brought an *end* to my holiday. Not only did I have to read the books, but watch all

12 No Monkeys in Heaven

the movies too, and there were twelve—one for each semester week.

On my return the following year in 2010, I patiently waded through lessons on biological evolution and natural selection, and then onto cultural evolution and adaptation. The powerpoint notes were well illustrated and easy to understand. Whatever questions I could not answer, I got back to the class on the next day. The rest was in the textbook. One phrase went something like this:

Once man had evolved from an ape, his intelligence and skills developed faster than his body could adapt to the environment, therefore man did not evolve to acquire fur like a polar bear because 'culture and technology' provided the necessary warmth. And that's when my patience ran out!

I asked them what they thought of the theory that humans evolved from hairy apes to naked men who need to make clothes to keep themselves warm. No one answered. Then I asked who believed that their ancestors were monkeys. They all put up their hand. I talked about the "Cambrian Explosion" as one of evolutions unexplained phenomenon, but no one had heard of it. So, I briefly touched on a few topics of creation that clearly required more analysis. Life forms that show, by their function, evidence of an intelligent designer:

"Bacterium flagellum, for example, is a single celled microorganism with a long tail (flagellum) that it uses to move around. It has the same parts and functions as an outboard motor. Both the bacterium and the out board motor need all their parts to function simultaneously. Therefore, the existence of the bacteria flagellum does not allow for the slow process of evolution, as it requires precision engineering to function as a complete organism.

"The slow evolution process would not have allowed a giraffe to survive either, as he needed a unique circulatory system to function from the time of his existence. The giraffe has a network of small blood vessels at the base of his brain that controls the blood flow and pressure to the brain when he bends his neck downward. Without these capillaries stopping the blood from rushing to his brain, the giraffe would have had a stroke. In addition, the giraffe has a series of one-way valves in the veins of his neck that enable him to lift his head up again without getting disorientated. Without the one-way valves in place, he would have collapsed in a dizzy spell. No other animal has this unique circulatory system.

"Another example of intelligent design is the eye. The intricate components of the eye work like a camera. When light passes through the lens of the eye, or camera, it is recorded on the back of the eye, or in the case of a digital camera, on a memory card. If the eye evolved, it would have taken millions, or even billions, of years before any animal could have had vision. Our creator intelligently designed animals with eyes to see from the time of their existences, just as man has used *his* intelligence to design the camera.

"The information in DNA is perhaps the best example of intelligent design. DNA is much like the letters of the alphabet that make up words. The English alphabet has 26 letters and uses many of the same letters to make up different words. DNA's alphabet has only 4 letters: A, T, C, G, and each codon (word) is always 3 letters long. Just as a string of English words make up a sentence, long lines of codons makes up genes, which gives us our unique identity. The mechanics and mathematics involved in the molecular structure of DNA demands intelligent composition not random selection."

The class was silent, so I continued:

"Now we know the outboard motor didn't evolve and neither did the camera. A dictionary didn't appear with an

12 No Monkeys in Heaven

explosion on the printing press—even a monkey could figure that out."

Everyone laughed. Then the bell rang and class was over. I felt that I had entertained them more than enlightened them when one of the boys came and thanked me for the lesson; he said it had given him something to think about.

Week after week, we carried on with cultures and subcultures, patriarchs and matriarchs, communication and religions ... and then my patience ran out again. The textbook promoted every major religion under the sun, *except* Christianity. The story of creation, the flood and Noah in the book of Genesis, were all used as examples of the world's greatest myths, and so was heaven.

Every ancient culture has a story of a worldwide flood and many allude to eight people in a boat. The students all knew this to be true and nodded their heads in agreement. I asked if they knew that heaven existed, who of them would want to go there. Again, they all raised their hand.

"Well, there're no monkey ancestors in heaven!" I had the freedom to speak and they had the freedom to listen.

I talked a bit about the flood and how God was grieved that He had made man. And, as the topic was on world religions, I gave them a lesson on mine. I cleaned the board and illustrated the fall of Adam into sin and God's plan of salvation through the sacrificial death of Jesus on the Cross.

In the days that followed, I waited for a reaction—a phone call, or an email summoning me to the office. Nothing happened. The students never reported it, not even the spy!

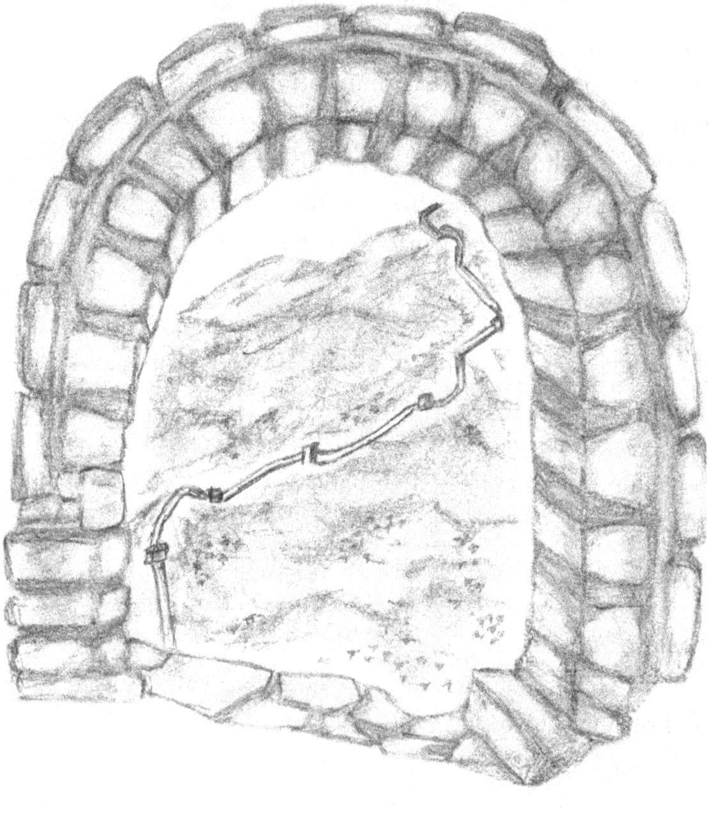

Mutianyu - Great Wall

13
Tombs and Travel Lessons

There is a friend who sticks closer than a brother.

Proverbs 18:24b

THE EASTER WEEKEND WAS TWO weeks away, and I heard that it was also a holiday in China: "Tomb Sweeping Day." That sounded intriguing, and who better to ask about it than Achilles—he was more than happy to explain.

"Qingming Festival" is a spring festival and a day to honour the ancestors. The tombs of their relatives are swept clean and the weeds around it are cleared. Food offerings, usually jiaozi (dumplings) are placed on the tomb together with paper money, which is burned. The money signifies prosperity for those in the afterlife.

"So what do *you* actually do, Achilles?" thinking that this would be an important ritual in his life.

"I stay at home and play computer games. My parents go to the tombs." He said with his mischievous smile.

"Well, *we* have a celebration about a tomb too," I continued, grasping another opportunity to tell him about the death and resurrection of Jesus and the "empty tomb" in Jerusalem. "Not every believer is able to visit the tomb, but we all remember the special day by getting together for communion, a meal of bread and wine. The bread symbolizes Christ's body, and the wine, His blood that was shed on the Cross. Because of this sacrifice, we have the promise of everlasting life. Our lives are blessed now, too, as the Bible promises that God will meet all our needs." Achilles nodded, impressed that we should have such an important day in common.

*****

The teachers took advantage of the long weekend for sightseeing. I was eager to see the Great Wall, so I planned a trip with three of my American friends: Sharon, Bryan, and Kate. Bryan was from Orange County and Kate from Oregon. We were all set to go, but plans seldom go smoothly in China! In fact, whenever someone asks me what life was like in China, I always answer the same, "China is a daily challenge!" Our challenge at that time was with our passports.

The college collected our passports for visa checks every new semester and sometimes kept them a couple of months. We had no idea why they held them for so long. Rumour had it that they were being used to purchase foreign cars. Foreigners were not permitted to travel in China without their passports, and no hotel would accommodate us unless we could produce one. So, until they were returned to us, we weren't going anywhere. We couldn't even book train tickets without a passport number.

Unscrupulous Innkeepers

Everyone complained, and the administrator assured us that all passports would be returned to us in time for the holiday. Our passports *were* returned in time, all except for

13 *Tombs and Travel Lessons*

one—Bryan's. We managed to book his train-ticket using a photocopy, but that was not going to hold at the hotel.

"Bring the photocopy; we'll find a way," Sharon said, she was used to these little difficulties. We arrived at our hotel on Friday night and checked in, and as expected, they refused Bryan's photocopy, and he had to look for another place to stay. Bryan went to several hotels and eventually found one that had a basement room with a mouldy ceiling and no ventilation. The unscrupulous hotel owner charged him double the price of a regular room to rent it. Bryan was determined not to let it spoil our weekend, and we all spent the Saturday happily exploring parts of the old town.

Dangerous, Pay Your Attention!

Sharon and Kate had other plans for Sunday, so Bryan and I took a long bus ride to Mutianyu, a section of the Great Wall that was not as frequently visited by tourists. A big sign told us that the left side of the wall was safe, and most of the visitors went left, but we wanted to avoid large groups, so we took the road less travelled, and turned right. We came face to face with another large sign:

"Dangerous Section—Pay Your Attention!" Everything in China comes with a fee—we paid our attention and continued on.

It was a still clear day and the view from the top stretched out for miles. We could see the wall snaking up and over the hills and across the valleys disappearing again on the horizon. A bright blue sky canopied this scenic vista with not a cloud in sight, or a hint of a breeze. We were very grateful, as navigating the wall, especially on treacherous parts, can be very tricky on windy days. We stood in silence for some time, just taking it all in. While we marvelled at the view it now freely gave us, I couldn't help but think of the lives that were sacrificed in its construction, and the untold suffering it had brought to the families of the victims. It was Resurrection Sunday and Tomb Sweeping Day—a time for contemplation.

Drama at the Station

On Monday morning, we were up early. Our train was scheduled to depart at 12:50 p.m., so we had the morning free. At around 11:15 a.m., we were relaxing in a restaurant in a shopping centre when I began to feel very uneasy. At 11:30, I suggested to the group that we should leave for the station. I felt something was about to go wrong and knowing the crowds we would encounter, I wanted to give us as much time as possible.

"We still have plenty of time. The station's not far from here and we have the tickets," Sharon said. She reached into her purse and handed three of the tickets to Kate. Then she stood up to leave the table for a last minute shop. Kate gave a ticket to Bryan and waved the other in my direction. I was just out of reach, so I told her to hold onto it, I would get it at the station. That was a big mistake. When traveling in a group, especially in China, each person should hold their own ticket; circumstances can change like the wind, and people can easily get separated in the overcrowding. We had previously discussed what we would do if we were split up, and where to meet if our phone connections failed, which often happened. Some networks only function in certain areas. If we found ourselves alone, our motto was, "Always take care of yourself!"

Sharon returned and she could see that I was still unsettled. She looked at her watch. We now had less than an hour. "Okay," she said. "Let's go."

13 Tombs and Travel Lessons

It was only a short taxi ride—that was, if you could get a taxi. The city was notorious for taxi drivers refusing foreigners. Many of the drivers could understand a little English, but they had little patience with foreigners. There were enough locals to keep them in business. The taxis whizzed by, and then Sharon managed to collar one that stopped to drop off a fare. She held open the back door to detain him and signalled for us to jump in. The three of us squashed in the back with our bags while Sharon got in the front. The driver refused to move and told us all to get out. Sharon spoke to him in Mandarin and then he became more cooperative. Still, he wouldn't take three in the back. He said it was too many with our bags, and one of us had to get out.

Sharon got out and told Bryan to get in the front. She would find another taxi and meet us at the entrance to the station. Sharon would have been fine on her own, she was acquainted with the city and spoke the language, but I wasn't thinking wisely and got out of the car.

"I'll go with you," I said, forgetting that Kate had my ticket.

We managed to hail another taxi, but time was running out. The main station had two entrances. Bryan and Kate's taxi dropped them off on one side, and our taxi dropped us off at the other. My phone signal was down, but Sharon's was still working. She called Bryan and told him to meet us at the clock—there were clocks on both sides. We stood on our toes to peer over hundreds of heads in the crowded hallway, but neither of us could see them.

"Call him again." I urged, but Sharon's signal had dropped as well, so she texted him to say that we were at the clock. He texted back, "So are we." Then Sharon realized what had happen.

"They're on the other side," she said. "There's no time to go around now, we must get through gate. We can meet up in the coach."

"Kate has my ticket," I winced.

"What?" She stopped and grabbed hold of my arm. "But, I gave you all your tickets."

"I know. I told Kate to hold onto mine."

Sharon looked at the clock. It was four minutes to departure; the gates had been open for six minutes already. The gates open ten minutes before the trains leave, and they *always* leave on time! You had exactly ten minutes to declare your passport and ticket, find the right platform, and board the train. After ten minutes, the boarding gates close, and so do the train doors. Many foreigners have been separated when this happens, and it always results in a panic. I had heard the stories from others, and I had had my own experience on my first train trip. I stopped to help one of the teachers with a small child who couldn't keep up. The coach door closed as we reached the train, but a feisty teacher on the inside pushed the guard out of the way and opened the door for us. She could have been thrown off the train for that.

A Friend in Need

"Come on!" Sharon, still holding onto my arm, pulled me along as she ran. We reached our boarding gate—it was still open. Sharon explained our dilemma to the guard in Mandarin and tried to persuade her to let us go through and get the ticket from Kate on the train. We would have to show our tickets on the train again, and those who did not have one would be made to get off at the next station. We would never have risked that if we didn't have a ticket, but the guard was not willing. We had run out of time; the train was about to depart in two minutes. Sharon grabbed my hand, shoved her ticket in it, and then pushed me through the gate.

13 Tombs and Travel Lessons

"Get on the first coach you see, you can find your way to your coach from the ticket number. You'll see the others there." I stared at her in disbelief. How could I walk away and leave her stranded when I was the one who didn't take my ticket? She gave me a reassuring smile. "I'll be fine, I'll find my way home, now get on the train."

I knew she was right. If I had been left behind alone, I certainly would not have coped. I had travelled alone in Europe, Turkey, and the UK, but this was China, a different part of the planet. I don't do well in crowds at the best of times, and many of China's cities are more populated than the whole of New Zealand. And, there are no English signs, or information centres.

I held up the ticket to the guard and then ran for the nearest coach and jumped on just as the train doors closed behind me. The train pulled out of the station as I pushed my way down the crowded isles from coach to coach, and then I saw Bryan and Kate already in their seats. There was no need to ask questions, they knew what had happened. I sat down, afraid to speak, and on the verge of tears.

"She'll be okay," Bryan said reassuringly. "You know Sharon, she's a tough traveller and she speaks the language."

We all knew that there were only two trains that day and they were both fully booked well in advance. We tried to call her repeatedly, but there was no signal, not even for a text. It was a long journey home.

Sharon did not live on campus; she rented her own apartment. We would have to wait until the next day to hear from her. I went to bed exhausted and prayed that she would be safe.

Early the next morning I received a text—she was home and safe. She had waited until our train departed to make certain I was on it. Then she went to the ticket office to see if there had been any cancelations on the later train. There were none, not even standing room, so she checked the flight times on the internet, took a taxi to the airport and booked a seat on the next available flight. We all chipped in to help pay for her fare.

14
An Angel in Intensive Care

For He shall give His angels charge over you, to keep you in all your ways.

Psalm 91:11

THE STUDENTS HAVE A SAYING about the weather in China. "Winter fell in love with summer and killed spring." The same applies for autumn. The seasons change very quickly from summer to winter and vice-versa. Temperatures can vary from 45° C in summer to minus 40° C in winter, in places. It's in these quick changes that we have to watch out for colds and flu. My second winter was soon upon us. When the icy winds cut through the campus, I seldom went out in the evenings.

I was late in returning from class one Friday afternoon and had just hung up my coat when the phone rang. Peter sounded very distressed. He asked me to pray for his youngest daughter, Cristina. She had contracted asthmatic pneumonia and was taken to the hospital. Cristina was nine years old and prone to asthma attacks. She usually overcame them, but this time it was far more serious.

"Of course I'll pray," I replied. "Which hospital is she in?" The minute I put down the phone I called Elle, a colleague and friend who was also a believer and an intercessor. She and her husband, Joseph, a medical doctor, had already heard the news and were contemplating going to the hospital. We agreed to meet and go together. I put on my coat again and slipped out the door to embrace the evening chill.

Fortunately, Joseph was acquainted with the children's hospital and was able to guide us through the maze of wards on every level to get to the intensive care unit. We arrived upstairs to find Peter and his wife standing outside the high-care ward. Visiting hours were over and no one was permitted to enter, not even the parents. Just then, a local doctor arrived. She was also a believer and a friend of the family. She assured us that everything was being done to save Cristina.

Cristina was in a critical condition and making it through the night was a real concern. The six of us stood outside the high-care ward until we were certain that no one else was around. Then we held hands and called on the Name of the Lord. While we were praying, I looked up to see the back of a very tall angel as he walked straight through the double doors and into the high-care ward.

"She's going to be all right," I exclaimed. "I've just seen an angel go through the door. She's not alone." The others sensed a peaceful presence too; then we all agreed that we should leave. Peter and his wife needed to rest after their exhausting ordeal. They could trust the Lord and His angel to take care of Cristina.

Cristina made it through the night and was soon released from the hospital and returned to her family. We prayed Psalm 91 over her every morning and every evening, but Peter's problems were not over yet. The hospital bill amounted to 13,000 RMB, a huge amount for a single income family. We prayed for that, too, and the Lord stretched out His hand

14 *An Angel in Intensive Care*

through the local believers who collected well over the required amount. What a faithful God we serve!

Psalm 91, for me, is "the miracle Psalm." Often, when I've prayed this Psalm over very ill people they have recovered quickly. It's a Psalm full of hope and promise, and it has worked miracles for believers in all kinds of difficult circumstances. J. R. Church, in his book, *Hidden Prophecies of the Psalms*, professes this Psalm to be prophetic of a remnant of Jewish people who will be saved during the Great Tribulation. [34]

15
Questions About Life

Always be ready to give a defence to everyone who asks you a reason for the hope that is in you, with meekness and fear.

1 Peter 3:15

ON MY NEXT HOLIDAY BREAK, Peter asked if I could get hold of ALPHA material to use for the English Corner.

"Wouldn't that be ministering to the students?" I asked.

"It's not for the locals," he assured me, "it's for the foreign students. In that way we can equip them to minister to the locals; they have more contact with them on a social level." There were hundreds of foreign students on our campus who came to learn Chinese and hundreds more on other campuses doing degrees in various subjects. It was a great idea!

I had befriended a pastor at a local Church in Auckland and I knew they ran the ALPHA course, so I approached him about obtaining the material. He told me that their courses were sent from Singapore. As one of his colleagues was in Singapore at that time, he called him and asked if he could bring ALPHA material with him on his return to New Zealand. His colleague returned to Auckland the day before my departure to China with the whole ALPHA course in English and Mandarin.

Peter was delighted and eager to start the first session. Sharon and I offered to assist. On the night of our first meeting, it wasn't only foreign students, but our own local students turned up as well. We discussed what to do. We did have the English version and we could make the first meeting an English study. We ran the first part of the video and then split up into smaller groups to discuss the lesson. It was a great opportunity for the students to improve their English and gain more insight into the meaning of life.

My English classes ran late on a Friday, so I was not able to continue with Alpha for long, but Peter and Sharon carried on with a regular turnout of seventeen students on the first course. Ten of them gave their hearts to the Lord by the seventh session, and seven out of thirteen got saved on the second course.

*****

My third semester was now coming to a close with another Christmas approaching. Simon would often text me with special prayer requests, and they were always answered beyond his expectations—his faith was growing. I shared my vision with him for a special Christmas outreach in the college foyer. He was keen to be involved, and as an accomplished musician, he offered to assist with the music. He wanted to play his saxophone with the carol singers.

I approached Peter once more; however, he was still concerned how the consequences might affect his family. I asked a few of the other teachers, and they too, declined. Sharon was interested, but we needed a bigger team. I reluctantly told Simon it was not God's plan at this time. I was disappointed, too. I had planned to stay for two years and this was my last

Christmas. I left for the holidays and returned again in the New Year. Early April was when the new contracts were signed and I had already told the office I would not be staying. I received an email asking me if I would reconsider and I felt a prompting within me to say yes. I hesitated; I had to be sure this was from the Lord. The two years I'd spent in China had taken its toll on my health. I was frequently taking antibiotics, and I wasn't the only one who suffered with health issues. The air pollution left everyone complaining of sinus headaches and chest infections. The bottled water delivered to our apartments often tasted foul, gastro bugs prevailed throughout the year, and the students would pass the flu around every winter. Some teachers never stayed more than a few weeks, others lasted one semester (3 months), and others one year. However, the peace that passes understanding is my general guide to all decision-making, and I definitely had this peace, so I signed up. If the Lord was saying stay, then He would see me through another year.

What about Christmas?

As each new semester year begins in September, I started my final year in 2012 with another Christmas just around the corner. This time it *would* be my last. Come October, I mentioned a Christmas outreach once more to my peers, but again no response. Sharon had left China to assist with a family crisis and would not be returning. I did not see how I could achieve this on my own, so once again, I put the matter out of my mind. Towards the end of November, Simon and I were walking to class when he broached the subject.

"What about the Christmas singing? This year is my last year and you too. It's our only chance."

"I know," I replied solemnly, "but no one's interested, and I can't blame them. It could have dangerous consequences for the people who are staying behind. They have their families to think of."

"No, it will be okay," Simon insisted, "it's not dangerous. God will help you. I can get some students to help, too." I had previously shared with Simon that God only needed one obedient person to work through; the Old Testament is full of stories of the "obedience of one." I laughed and told him that this time there needed to be more than one or two, as there would be many students asking questions. Christmas time always heightened curiosity about God: "Is Christmas the same as Easter?" "Is Jesus and Santa the same person?" "Why do we have a tree and presents?" "What's Christmas Eve about?" "What do we do on Christmas day?" The questions were the same every year. They knew nothing of the petroglyphs discovered in 1980 showing the Nativity of the first century believers.

I believe the answers never satisfied because they did not have a real experience to fortify them. This outreach could give them that; it could open a door for the Holy Spirit to touch their lives. Christmas time gives us a great opportunity to evangelize.

I didn't feel too excited at the prospect, though, as I had given up, but it was only "the darkness before the dawn." Simon and I walked up the steps and into the large foyer where we both stopped dead in our tracks.

"The chairs are gone!" he blurted out in surprise.

"Yes, and the place looks so empty," I responded. All the heavy lounge chairs that once spread across the hallway had been removed. It left the whole foyer wide open. There was more than enough standing room for over a hundred students.

Every year the college puts up a large Christmas tree for the foreign teachers. I asked Simon to check with security that the tree was still going up.

"Yes," he said, returning with a big smile, "and they're putting up two this year." My heart quickened as hope returned.

"Go speak to Peter," Simon insisted, "one more time!"

I found Peter alone in his office and approached my subject carefully.

"Did you notice all the chairs downstairs have been removed?" I asked him.

"Yes, I did," he replied. And before he could say any more, I went on to explain.

"Simon asked me to ask you one more time. He feels this is a God idea, and we should give it a try. And, he's more than willing to help with the music, and will even get other students involved for whatever we need." This time Peter smiled and resigned himself to the fact that I was not going to give up.

"Okay, but we need to work out very carefully what we are going to do, and how we are going to present this to management. Don't be surprised if we get turned down."

A Favour in Return

We prayed and planned, and prayed again. We decided that Peter would be the one to talk to management, as he had been there the longest. Should the reply come back negative, it would be final. The authorities never change their minds.

The college was open to cultural events and, at times, invited students from other colleges to participate in sports and the arts. Peter presented our request as a cultural event and explained how, at Christmas time each year, the students always asked the same questions. We could share why we celebrate Christmas, sing a few songs, and hand out candy with goodwill verses attached.

To our surprise, the response was positive, providing we did only what we said we would do and nothing else, that is, no preaching or praying, and no one outside of our campus could participate. Our next step would be to clear this with the Head of Department, and for this, we would need a written permit. I was to collect an official letter later that week and take it to the Dean for further authorization.

Peter couldn't help with this as his Mandarin was weak and the Dean's English was weaker still. I presented my case to our administration lady who assisted us with all our complaints and queries. She spoke English well, and listened to my appeal with interest. She also understood the confusion that Christmas brought to the Chinese students.

"We have to get the final signature from the Dean," I pleaded. "He won't understand me."

She thought for a moment. "Don't worry," she said. "You did a big favour in helping us with the syllabus."

There is a custom in China that if you do someone a favour, then you should receive one in return, and the favour in return must equal the one given.

She stood up, took the permit from me and walked out of the office. The wheels of protocol turn very slowly in China. I was expecting a long wait, or to be told to return another day. To my surprise, she was back in a few minutes, smiling and waving the paper at me.

"I reminded him of how you helped us with the syllabus. He didn't ask any questions."

The next step was to take the letter to security, but she promised to call them and instruct them to assist us in whatever we needed. God knew about the custom in China and He had prepared in advance for me to be granted a favour. With God, nothing is impossible. He is faithful to complete that which He said He would do.

Han Dynasty Stone Relief Museum

16
The Culture of Christmas

*Not by might nor by power, but by My Spirit,
says the LORD of Hosts.*

Zechariah 4:6

OUR OUTREACH WAS SCHEDULED TWO days before Christmas. It was exam time, which meant that there were few afternoon classes and most of the students would be free. Peter promised to bring along his family who were all very musical. I called Elle and Joseph as they were good singers, and Simon recruited two more students to help with the decorating. One other foreign teacher offered to help with answering questions. It was a busy time of year with finals and other cultural events, so we only managed one music practice together, but Simon met with me every week to master his carol playing on the saxophone. We had permission to post notices in all the nearby student apartments and on the college notice boards.

Dragon, of course, wasn't at all happy about our plans. Doubts were raised from the non-participant believers about the risks we would be subjecting everyone to and the disastrous consequences that would ensue. Naturally speaking, they were right, but this was not a natural event. We knew God had His protective hand over it, but that doesn't mean that everything always goes smoothly.

A few days before the outreach, things started to unravel. Elle and Joseph had to withdraw due to other more pressing commitments in their fellowship. I was at a loss as to who was going to lead the singing. I had come down with a cold and a sore throat, and by the morning of the outreach, my throat was quite inflamed. I groaned at the prospect of trying to speak, let alone sing. It was 7 a.m. and I was expected to be in the foyer by nine. Simon had arranged for two students to help. We had already given them all the decorations; I knew they would attend to it.

At 8 a.m. I received a very cheerful call from Bright, a foreign student from off campus. Elle had told him about our event and asked if he would help. Bright was a keen singer. He had written a song for the Christmas season and was eager to share it with the world. There was just one problem—he was not from our campus!

"I'm so sorry," I replied hoarsely. We really do need your help, but we're not allowed to have off campus students involved.

"No problem. I'll come anyway, just to watch," he replied. He was not deterred. I gave him directions and promised to meet him at the main gate if he left immediately. He arrived in time and then we met up with Peter and his family at the entrance to the foyer. Peter was delighted to see Bright. Everyone was in good spirits. Two large partitions beautifully decorated with pictures of the Nativity stood between two tall Christmas trees. In front, were three tables covered in red paper with candles and a portable speaker had been placed on each table. The Christmas tree lights were flashing to add to the festivities.

16 The Culture of Christmas

The Reason for the Season

There was no point trying to sing. I turned off my mike and picked up my guitar. At least I could play. The foyer doors kept opening and closing, letting in the cold air and the temperature in the foyer dropped. My fingers froze, until I found that I couldn't play all the cords. I tried to stay calm. Peter's daughter played guitar—I had a backup. Simon played sax, and we had two more singers, but I wasn't prepared for what happened next. Bright, sensing the need for a lead vocalist picked up a mike and proceeded to sing with gusto. More students gathered around.

In no time at all the hallway was packed with spectators, and Bright, a foreign student, was leading the singing. Out the corner of my eye, I noticed one of the security guards make his way over to us. For a moment, I felt that all our hard work and prayers were going to end in disaster. I knew we could be stopped at any time. The guard walked around us and then went back to his desk. The singing ended and Peter took up a mike and began to share the reason for Christmas. This could have been constituted as preaching. Staying calm was becoming more difficult. I put down my guitar and went behind the partition to pray. Perhaps it was the onset of the flu, or just my carnal fears, but in my anxiety, I prayed the "Adam" kind of prayer, "Oh Lord, this was *Your* idea, *You* told me to do this, now *we* could all be arrested." The Lord was not concerned. The next thing I heard was Bright singing even louder. It was the special song he had written for Christmas, and the chorus line was, "Jesus is the reason for the season." He seemed to have forgotten all the verses as he repeated, "Jesus is the reason for the season," over and over, and over again.

I thought he was going to have the Head of Department and the whole Chinese staff down in a minute. Oh, me of little faith! I resigned to the fact that the Lord was in control, and not me, so I came out from behind the partition and joined in, wondering how we were all going to testify at the police station later that day.

Some of the students left with Bright's proclamation, but those who stayed, stayed until the end, and even then, they didn't want to leave. They asked Bright to teach them a song that they could sing along, and very soon, *Feliz Navidad* went out across the foyer as all the students joined in. We handed out candy with "God Loves You" labels and answered all their questions. When it was time to pack up, a few of the students remained behind to help and asked us if they could visit with us another day. They were keen to know more. We met off campus in a rather nice hotel where I celebrated my first Chinese Christmas lunch. And their first Christmas lunch ever. This was a new experience for them and they had many questions. I answered them carefully, as it was still a public place. The English corners grew as a result of the outreach, and more students came to know the Lord.

Every opportunity

We don't always know the full results of the Lord's work in our ministry. When we are sent out in the fields to work, it's often others who come behind to reap the harvest. Over the years, I have come to accept that the results belong to God. My job is to obey His instructions and leave the outcome with Him. I felt very blessed that a miracle had occurred that day, in bringing the Gospel to a people who were forbidden to hear it, in a place that forbade any kind of evangelism. Yet, many eyes had been opened and seeds planted and students had come to know Jesus. The Lord had indeed answered the desires of my heart that He placed there when I was just a young woman.

16 *The Culture of Christmas*

*****

Although we now know that the birth of Jesus was not on December 25th, but more than likely during Nissan [35] on the Hebrew calendar, which would be March/April on our Western calendar, December 25th gives us the opportunity to present the Gospel to those who would not otherwise hear it. The Great Commission is to go out into the world, and not to hide away from it. We need to celebrate Jesus every day, and take every opportunity to share the Good News.

Dragon's Head
Shanhaiguan

17
Leaving the Land of Dragon

I press toward the goal for the prize of the upward call of God in Christ Jesus.

Philippians 3:14

MY CONTRACT WAS COMING TO an end again, and this time, I felt a prompting from the Lord to prepare to leave. With Sharon gone and Simon graduating, it made it easier to move on. Bryan had already left and so had Kate. With each stop on the journey one always forges friendships, but it's only a matter of time, when new friends continue on their way and you're left standing as though in a void. Home was never an option for me. The missionaries I met on my travels all cautioned me with the same words: "Once you've left your homeland, you're always a sojourner." Those who return on furlough, or to repatriate, find the changes that have taken place while they were away often leave them feeling like foreigners in their own country. It's one way the Lord keeps us out of a comfort-zone, and thankful for any little comfort that does come our way.

My visa application for New Zealand was now in the queue and it would not be processed until later that year. Every time I prayed for direction, England came to mind. My ancestral visa for the UK had long since expired and to complicate matters, the British immigration department had extended their requirements on renewals. To obtain the necessary documents, I would have to return to South Africa. Anyone who has ever battled with the South African Home Affairs will know the difficulties involved. If something goes wrong, and invariably it does, it takes the hand of God to intervene to put it right. Besides, I was weary of protocol. I had just spent the best part of two years getting the New Zealand immigration papers in order. Obtaining clearance certificates in China proved as difficult as extracting a tooth from a tiger. I knew I could not face dealing with more complex visa applications, plus there was no guarantee that I would get the documents I needed. Either I must be hearing wrong, or the Lord had another plan in getting me through UK customs.

William Cowper once stated in a hymn he wrote, "The Lord works in mysterious ways His wonders to perform." My first mysterious sign came in a dream. My late Swiss father appeared to me with an encouraging smile. I awoke wondering what it could mean. It was the first time I had dreamt of him since his death; it had to be significant, and it didn't take long to find out. That same week I had a dream about my nephew in London. I emailed him to tell him. When he replied, he told me that he had been searching the Swiss registry to see who in the family was still listed, and he had found my name there.

I had previously lost my dual nationality, but my name was never removed from the Swiss database. In 2006, the Swiss government had changed their policy on Swiss nationals born outside of Switzerland. Those who were still registered were now considered nationals again. I called the Swiss consulate in China and waited with bated breath. "Yes, you are a citizen.

17 Leaving the Land of Dragon

You can have a Swiss passport," a voice said at the other end—I could hardly believe my ears.

With only a few online forms to fill in, plus the standard fee for travel documents, I was soon off to the embassy to collect my new passport and praised God for the efficiency of the Swiss!

I attended Simon's graduation and we promised to stay in touch—he was off to do further studies in the USA and I was to end up in New Zealand, eventually. On the day of my departure, Joseph and Elle and a few of my students came to say goodbye. "Don't worry," Simon said, encouragingly, "Wherever you are in the world, I will come and visit you."

Backlash from Dragon

Leaving China proved to be another battle—Dragon wasn't letting me out easily. After a six hour wait at International Departures, it was announced that our flight would be delayed for a further twenty-four hours. I felt distraught. My mobile phone wouldn't work in the airport, and I needed to contact my nephew in London who would be waiting for me in vain. An airport official tapped me on the shoulder and bent over close to my ear.

"Do you need help?" he whispered. "I see you are wearing a cross. That means you're a Christian. I'm a Christian, too. I'd like to help you." He whispered again.

"It's my phone. I can't get a connection," I replied, thankful that I had chosen to wear my cross to the airport, not something I usually do off campus in China.

"Here, you can use mine," he said, and handed his phone to me with a smile. "Take your time. I'll be over there." He pointed in the direction he would be and left me to it.

The Lord never leaves us nor forsakes us, especially in foreign lands. I have often felt stranded—when I got lost or missed my bus stop or boarded the wrong train—only to find help right by my side. One day we will know if they were real people or angels sent to guide us on our journey.

I made my call, returned the phone, and then booked into a nearby hotel to wait it out. The airlines offered to pay one night's accommodation per person. However, the hotel did not offer single rooms. I was forced to pay for the second half of a double room. The following morning, after another four-hour delay, two of which were on the runway waiting for take-off—I was finally air-born and England bound. I looked out the window as we rose above the clouds and I thought I saw the backlash of a giant dragon's tail.

Tower Bridge, London

18
The Next Step

I press on, that I may lay hold of that for which Christ has also laid hold of me.

Philippians 3:12

WITHIN THE FIRST FEW WEEKS on arrival in England in June 2012, several things went through my mind about my purpose for being there, but uppermost was revival. I had heard about a Scottish evangelist, who started a 70-day walk in the shape of a cross over Britain. I followed his trail and I was encouraged by the attention and positive response he was getting.

I started a job search on the internet and came across an offer to attend a two-day life-coaching seminar with a coaching academy in the heart of London. It certainly caught my attention, and I wondered if the Lord used the internet for direction—He once used a donkey. I filled in an online form and was secured a place. My nephew was interested too, so the two of us went along to find out what life coaching was all about.

In the years I had spent as a Christian counsellor in South Africa, I had often wondered how those who came for counselling had progressed on their journey. Once the counselling sessions were over, they would return to their fellowships and get on with their lives, and I would often never hear from them again. Without vision, the Scripture tells us,[36] we are at risk of slipping back to old habits and patterns. Counselling alone was not sufficient. There needed to be "a next step."

As I listened to the precepts and pathways to coaching, it resonated within my spirit. Where counselling serves to shape values and beliefs, coaching brings purpose into focus and bridges the gap between vision and the realisation of the final goal. Although we cannot find any evidence of coaching in the Scriptures, the principles and practices of the Bible can certainly be found in life coaching. It encourages people to set time-bound goals for which they can be accountable. I found this very inspiring and thought it could well be the next step!

After only two days, I was convinced and ready to take up the challenge with one, not so small problem—the fees were out of my reach. Converting Chinese RMB to BSS (British Sterling Silver) requires a big adjustment in the budget.

The Coaching Academy offered a part-scholarship and invited those who needed assistance to apply. I filled in the form and left it in the Lord's hands, knowing that if He had brought me here, He would complete the purpose. Finding work proved even more difficult as most of the temporary teaching posts were taken prior to my arrival in England, so I called up the home care agency and returned to relief caring, which meant more travel.

God's Hand in all Circumstances

Two months later, I received an email to inform me that my application was being considered. They requested a one-page letter stating why I felt I should be nominated. Knowing that I

18 The Next Step

have an enemy that always interferes, I left nothing to chance. *In the multitude of counsellors there is safety.* [37]

I had planned a weekend trip to Bristol to visit with some friends, and thought it a good opportunity to seek advice. We prayed for the Holy Spirit's influence on the letter, and once everyone was satisfied with it, I emailed it to the academy. Within two weeks, I received a reply. I had been selected for the scholarship. Once again, I witnessed the hand of God in my circumstances and God's faithfulness shone through. He knows the plans He has for us and keeps us on the path—Hallelujah!

Scriptures in Secular Seminars

The completion of the course included six seminars, and I needed to attend a minimum of five before leaving the UK. I had no idea how much longer my New Zealand visa would take to process, so I worked fervently to get through all the course requirements in time.

The seminars were also spread across the country and I often found myself travelling four hours, changing trains twice, to sit through an eight-hour talk, and then another four hours travel home. And, that was in between the care work, which, in one year, covered the North, South, East and West of England and across to Wales.

Things worth doing for the Kingdom of God always come with a price.

> *For which of you, intending to build a tower, does not sit down first and count the cost, whether he has enough to finish it.*
> — Luke 14:28

Through every presentation, my mind filled with Scriptural references and to my surprise, a few were up on the power point—without direct reference of course!

Whatever things are true, whatever things are noble, whatever things are just, whatever things are pure, whatever things are lovely, whatever things are of good report, if there is any virtue and if there is anything praiseworthy--meditate on these things.
— Philippians 4:8

This could work for anyone and in any arena of life, but especially for the Kingdom of God. It could assist those who want to achieve more for God's purposes. Vision and an action plan with time-bound goals were the keys to accomplishment. It was easy to recognize Scriptural instruction in that:

- vision (Proverbs 29:18a)
- action plan – count the cost (Luke 14:28)
- progression in time-bound goals (Philippians 3:12)
- accountability (James 1:22)

Seek out the Intercessors

As with the counselling practicum, coaching required practical sessions with evaluations reports, which meant, I had to find people to coach. This proved even more challenging than travelling to the seminars. Most people are not aware of the benefits of personal coaching. Not being on my home ground, and having no social network, made it an even more difficult task. I prayed and asked the Lord to bring me people to coach, and instead, I felt led to seek out the intercessors. There was a small prayer group who met each week at the local church that I attended between travels.

Three ladies were present at my first meeting and they were more than happy for me to join in. When it came to my turn to present my request, I told them of my need and explained a little of how coaching would assist people from thinking about a dream or goal, to actually attaining it. Each woman sitting there had been incubating a dream she thought she could never realize. The reply from all of them was, "You can coach me!" Once again, the Lord proved faithful to supply the need. Coaching proved very effective and soon doors were opening for me to coach missionaries in China and Africa with great results.

Counting the Cost for the Sake of the Cross

On my journey I met people whose lives were changed by circumstances and events outside of their control, and this, as I said previously, always made me realize how small my problems and challenges were in comparison to the things others had to deal with. In Sutton, South of London, I met a young Saudi Arabian woman who was interested in being coached. She had counted the cost of converting to Christianity and paid a price that those of us who live in democratic countries never have to pay—forsaking *all* to follow Christ. Judy shared with me how she had to flee her country to escape arrest from the 'Religious Police' when it was discovered that she had converted to Christianity.

The penalty for leaving Islam for another religion is death. Judy found asylum in the UK and was never again to return to her family. Her quick escape gave her no time to prepare psychologically for a permanent migration, leaving behind all things familiar: family, friends and culture, and without even saying goodbye to her mother. She was an inspiration of courage, having gone from being a devout Muslim, who by the age of eleven had memorized three quarters of the Qur'an, to a committed Christian, now living by the Word of Faith. We soon became good friends and I agreed to work with her to publish her story.

Perfect Timing

My New Zealand visa took longer than expected, but was divinely held back, because more surprises were in store. The following year, April 2013, I received a skype call from my daughter in Australia. She knew of my life-long dream to visit Israel and the Lord had laid it on her heart to sponsor my trip. "It's time!" she said. And the timing was perfect! A Christian tour group had scheduled a ten-day archaeological trip and there was still a place open. I often imagined how intriguing it would be to visit Israel and walk the steps that Jesus had walked and visit all the Gospel sites, but an archaeological tour that visited many of the Old Testament sites, as well, was more than I had hoped.

In recent years, a lot more evidence has been uncovered attesting to the arrival of the Israelites in Canaan and their life and wars during the reigns of the kings of Israel and Judah. The itinerary with our Christian tour group covered many of these newly discovered places.

19
Chaos and Cancelled Flights

And we know that all things work together for good to those who love God, to those who are the called according to His purpose.

Romans 8:28

My TRIP WAS SCHEDULED TO leave on Good Friday and Heathrow airport was packed to the hilt. I found my group and waited with them for our boarding passes. The minutes passed into hours listening to the frequent announcements on delays and cancellations. We were due to board and still no gate numbers were up, and no sign of boarding tickets. I had an uneasy feeling that we were among the setbacks that night. It was well over our boarding time when our group leader, Paul came to break the news—our flight had been cancelled. The plane we were to take had punctured a tire on landing in Amsterdam and was now stranded there. Air-traffic was on a tight schedule with no space to accommodate an untimely plane once the tire was changed.

Our party of forty was to be divided up and put on any other available fights. We all stood motionless listening for our names and stepping up to receive a boarding pass. I was assigned with a party of ten to take the Frankfurt flight and the plane was scheduled for departure in less than twenty minutes. Boarding usually closed twenty minutes before take-off, but due to the cancellation, they agreed to hold the gates open for another five minutes. There was no time to check-in our luggage. We had to leave everything with one of our group leaders and run to get through customs.

The thought occurred to me that we might not see our luggage again with all the confusion, but, at that point, it didn't matter. I had waited over 30 years to visit Israel. I was going to enjoy it even if I had to wear the same clothes every day!

The Frankfurt flight was now five minutes past boarding, and I was at the end of a very long queue. When it came to my turn to pass through the scanner, the buckles on my boots set off the alarm. (Taking off shoes is not a requirement in all places.) I froze for moment, annoyed with myself for not thinking about that earlier, then quickly pulled off my boots and went through again. They weren't satisfied. I had to stand for a frisking while hopelessly watching everyone else in my party race into the departure lounge. Trying to hurry the inspection by telling them my flight was about to leave, didn't help either. They had heard that one too often. They simply shook their heads at me and took their time. If I didn't make it before boarding closed no one would know. I felt as though the enemy was trying to steal my trip, and I was on the brink of panic when at last they let me go.

I took off down the terminal without first closing my backpack. As I turned a corner, I looked over my shoulder to see the trail I was leaving behind—I hesitated for a snap decision. *Forfeit it all and carry on,* was my first thought—things weren't worth missing my flight.

19 Chaos and Cancelled Flights

"My camera!" I exclaimed. "Lord, send an angel to hold that plane," I shouted, as I dived for the camera and scooped up all my other belongings within reach, once again obstructing the flow of foot-traffic. This was not a good start to a life-long dream.

The captain was standing at the top of the flight stairs when I finally boarded. With his gold-winged badge on his blazer, he looked like an angel to me.

"Are you the last?" He asked with a big smile.

"Water," was my feeble reply. I felt like I was about to faint. He thought that was amusing, too.

From Frankfort, we changed planes for Jerusalem. This time I took off my boots and sent them through security on a tray. The rest of our tour group went via Brussels, Amsterdam, Vienna, and Zurich. When I heard that our baggage was flying Swiss Air via Zurich, I was confident it would all arrive safely in Jerusalem.

Empty Tomb

20
The Garden Tomb

Now to Him who is able to do exceedingly abundantly above all that we ask or think, according to the power that works in us.

Ephesians 3:20

OUR PARTY ON THE FRANKFURT flight was the first to arrive in Jerusalem late Saturday afternoon. I was delighted to find our Hotel only a few minutes' walk from the Old City Wall with the Garden Tomb just around the corner. I checked out my room and found the window overlooked a graveyard. Two men crouching behind a large white headstone were locked in conversation. I watched them for a while wondering what kind of deal was going down, until one of the men looked up at me. Immediately both men fled. I only hoped that stumbling on this clandestine encounter did not misconstrue me for a spy. Fair skinned foreigners are easily identified in the market places. Having had no bags to unpack I went in search of the Garden, and soon found myself standing before the empty tomb.

"He Is Not Here—For He Is Risen," the sign on the door stated. Up until that point, the events of the past twenty-four hours were still racing through my mind. Now, all was quiet. I scanned my surroundings, and then looked back at the opening in the rock, slowly processing exactly where I was. After all these years, my prayers were finally answered and I was in Jerusalem and standing in the Garden Tomb. This is the most likely site, according to Biblical accounts, where they had laid the body of Jesus and the place where He rose from the dead. I stood and watched quietly as a number of people entered and exited the tomb. I didn't feel I wanted to go in that day, so I walked along the little pathways that weaved around the flowerbeds.

The garden was much bigger than I had imagined and very well cared for. This was not a new discovery as the whole site had been excavated in 1867 when an ancient winepress and a well had been uncovered, but for me, it was as though it had all been revealed yesterday. I strolled along a pathway that led to the edge of the garden overlooking a huge rocky escarpment. There was something different about this vertical rock—it resembled a face with depressions for the eyes, nose and mouth. *Could this be Golgotha*, I thought. The tomb site is still a debate among archaeologist today, but this image on this rock-face cannot be ignored. It is the only skull-like rock-face ever discovered in Israel, and as it's widely known as the "Place of the Skull," it certainly points to the site where Jesus was crucified.

John's Gospel gives a clearer account: *Now in the place where He (Jesus) was crucified there was a garden, and in the garden a new tomb in which no one had yet been laid. So there they laid Jesus, because of the Jews' Preparation Day, for the tomb was nearby.* [38]

Matthew's Gospel account tells us that Joseph of Arimathea was given the body of Jesus: *When Joseph had taken the body, he wrapped it in a clean linen cloth, and laid it in his new tomb which he had hewn out of the rock; and he rolled a large stone against the door of the tomb, and departed.* [39]

20 The Garden Tomb

Isaiah tells that the suffering servant's grave was with the rich.[40] Joseph of Arimathea was a member of the Jewish council and a rich man.[41] A first century garden with a winepress and water-well, one of the largest in Jerusalem, would have belonged to a very wealthy man.

Resurrection Morning

Our baggage was delivered at 4 a.m. the following morning; I had time to freshen up before breakfast. I was thankful for having been on the earlier flight as it was Resurrection Sunday and there would be a special service at the Garden Tomb.

Chairs were spread out across the garden facing the empty tomb and they were fast filling up. Flags, representing the many nations that frequented the garden, were hoisted from one end to the other. There was a feeling of anticipation and excitement as everyone greeted each other. We were strangers and travellers from different lands, but there in the garden, we were all one in Christ. Little wooden cups and wafers were distributed as the Scriptures were read in various languages.

I looked around to see the fruit of the "Great Commission"; believers who had come from all over the world to offer up praise and thanksgiving to the Risen Lord. Together we took of the sacraments in remembrance of the Last Supper and the ultimate sacrifice. Alone and a stranger amongst a throng of foreigners, I felt an usual sense of unity and peace. They were, after all, my spiritual family, the people I would one day see again in Heaven. And, they felt it too—there was hardly a dry eye in the service that day.

Exploring the Old City

We set out early the following morning to Zedekiah's cave. Deep below the Old City lies a natural cave enlarged into a stone quarry. As I descended the slippery steps into the vast empty chambers, I imagined the cantabile cries of hundreds of King Solomon's men as they worked, cutting and chiselling the giant blocks of granite and then hauling them up to the mount to build the Temple walls.

Many of the buildings of Jerusalem were constructed with stone from this quarry, from its earliest inception in 3,000 B.C. Later, Suleiman, the Ottoman Sultan (1537 A.D.), built the Damascus Gate and the present wall that surrounds the Old City. I had more respect for the labourers of the Western Wall when I later stood beside the massive stones.

From the quarry we embraced the waters of Hezekiah's Tunnel. 2 Kings 20:20 and 2 Chronicles 32:2-4 record the threat of an Assyrian siege and the hasty construction of a tunnel dug to divert the flow of water from the Gihon Spring outside the city wall to the Pool of Siloam within.

With the hum of Indiana Jones' theme song from the more intrepid male explorers, we waded through waist high waters, stopping only to observe the ancient 'Siloah Inscription' placed by Hezekiah 2,700 years ago.

When we finally exited at the Pool of Siloam, I was ready to go back to the other side and do it all again, but Paul was heading for the recently excavated steps that led up to the Temple Mount and everyone obediently followed behind. We stopped near the mount, bordering the Kidron Valley, at the ruins of the ancient city of King David, another major archaeological discovery. Five layers of the city's remains now uncovered, revealing key periods of Biblical History, from the time of the Jebusites who first built it, to King David, 1,000 B.C.

20 The Garden Tomb

The Mount of Olives

Across the Kidron Valley to the Mount of Olives we climbed the hill and came to the place where Jesus rested with His disciples. Seeing the gnarled and twisted trunks of the age-old olive trees and knowing that Jesus had walked among them brought a reverent silence to the whole place. Whether the trees were the original trees or not, did not detract from the sanctity of the grove and the knowledge that this was where Jesus wrestled in prayer the night before the crucifixion. *"Father, if it is Your will, take this cup away from Me, nevertheless not My will, but Yours be done."* [42]

The little Tear Drop Chapel was filled with worshipers. People were coming and going from every angle of the garden, but everyone moved about quietly and respectfully. A monk appeared and walked among the trees, his long robe and tassels authenticating the scene.

When we descended the steep slope of the Mount, it struck me that we could be walking the very path that will one day be parted.

"Is this the mount that's going to be split in two?" I checked with our leader. He nodded and reminded us of the Scripture.

And in that day His feet shall stand on the Mount of Olives, which faces Jerusalem on the east. And the Mount of Olives shall be split in two, from east to west making it a very large valley; half of the mountain shall move toward the north and half of it toward the south. — Zechariah 14:4

The geological institute in Tel Aviv discovered a major fault line running right through the Mount of Olives. The Jerusalem earthquake of 1927 caused significant damage, reaching 6.2 on the Richter scale. The epicentre was in the northern part of the Dead Sea, which is directly in line with Jerusalem. Geologists at Tel Aviv University suggest that the region's next significant quake is now long overdue. [43]

The Golden Gate directly before us looked majestic. The only gate giving access to the Temple Mount and the one Messiah is expected to enter through, is also strategically placed on the path of the fault line before the Mount of Olives.

> *And the glory of the Lord came into the temple by way of the gate which faces towards the east.* — Ezekiel 43:4

> *Then He brought me back to the outer gate of the sanctuary which faces toward the east, but it was shut. And the Lord said to me, "This gate shall be shut; It shall not be opened, and no man shall enter by it, because the Lord God of Israel has entered by it; therefore it shall be shut."* — Ezekiel 44:1-2

Wailing Wall

On our visit to the Western Wall, I was permitted into the women's quarter, but I felt I was intruding and stopped only for a minute. I walked backwards to the entrance, as no woman ever turned her back on the Wall. The men coming up from their daily prayers, marching in rows of three and four and looking straight ahead, chanting as they made their way through the crowds of onlookers. There were young boys among the stalwart and resolute faces calling out chanting along with the men. A familiar wave of sadness crept over me. I knew I had heard these chants before ... outside the Synagogues in the Old Jewish Quarter in Prague, although, here in Jerusalem, the sadness was coupled with hope: *"All Israel shall be saved,"* the Apostle Paul had said (Romans 11:26).

I looked up above the Wall to Mount Moriah, the place where Abraham offered up his son Isaac, a shadow and type

20 The Garden Tomb

of the Saviour that was to come, and then later the Temple Mount, where Solomon's Temple once stood. It's now the home of the Dome of the Rock, a Moslem sanctuary, presiding over all of Jerusalem. Jesus said that He would not come a second time until Jerusalem acknowledges Him as their Messiah.

> *"Oh Jerusalem, Jerusalem, the one who kills the prophets and stones those who are sent to her! How often I wanted to gather your children together, as a hen gathers her chicks under her wings, but you were not willing! ... for I say to you, you shall see Me no more till you say, 'Blessed is He who comes in the name of the Lord!'"* — Matthew 23:37-39

Alone in the Garden

I had no desire to enter the Moslem temple, so when the others dispersed at the Mount, I slipped away from the group and meandered back down through the markets towards the Damascus Gate. My destination was the Garden Tomb, and hopefully, it would not be too crowded.

It was late afternoon when I entered the garden, and to my surprise, no one was around—I quietly stepped inside the Tomb.

The cool stone chamber was empty, yet full of peace. It was large enough for more than one person, but only one person had used it, and only for three days. "He is not here—for He is Risen," the sign on the door reminded me that the whole Christian faith rests on that one statement.

> *If Christ is not risen, your faith is futile; you are still in your sins!* — Corinthians 15:17

The twitter of birds drifted in from the outside, and then, all was still. My heart filled with gratitude for the hope of the resurrection and for the privilege of standing in the very place where Jesus had risen, and given those who would receive Him, the promise of eternal life.

Looking out through the Tomb doorway stood a tall tree with two branches extending at equal opposite ends. The two lateral branches had been cut back and stripped of foliage. The tree looked remarkably like a large wooden cross right in front of the Tomb. I was later told by one of the gardeners that this tree had been a witness to many, including Rabbis, who came out of curiosity to visit the tomb.

Megiddo

21

From Bethlehem to Megiddo

I am the Alpha and the Omega, the Beginning and the End.

Revelation 1:8a

BETHLEHEM IS ONLY A TWENTY-MINUTE drive from the Old City of Jerusalem in the territory of the West Bank. Our hotel was right opposite part of the "Separation Wall"; the younger members of the group were eager to take pictures. It was late, and I had seen enough political graffiti in Prague, so I turned in for the night.

The West bank, besides being the place of many Jewish and Christian Holy sites (the Cave of the Patriarchs in Hebron and the birthplace of King David and Jesus in Bethlehem), is also a strategic site of protection for Israel. I'm told that seventy percent of Israel's population would be in rocket range, if not for the West Bank. The Psalms tell us to pray for the peace of Jerusalem. [44] The following day I was to learn of the plight of those who live along the West Bank that protects Jerusalem.

Blood Brothers

Our first stop after breakfast the next morning was a little Christian book shop on the main street of Bethlehem and then on to the Bethlehem Bible College. I was eager to learn of how a Christian college survived in an area of so much political unrest.

The Dean shared the history of the college as well as the history of his family. He testified to being a descendant of a long line of Christians that he believed led back to the day of Pentecost. He showed us many pictures of his forefathers and relayed stories of the struggles of the Christian Palestinians, many of whom are now separated by the wall. He shared how in times of crisis, the small community behind the wall came together. Moslem believers would call on him for prayer when children became ill in the night, or mothers ran out of infant milk formula, things we take for granted in our Western culture with 24-hour emergency rooms and pharmacies.

"We know God answers your prayers!" They would say, and God always did.

As he spoke, I recalled a book I had once read by a Palestinian Christian, Elias Chacour. The title, *"Blood Brothers,"* relates to the common ancestry Jews and Arabs share in their Patriarch Abraham. The story was an account of the sufferings of the Palestinians during WWII. Elias' aim was to foster forgiveness and reconciliation among all peoples of his homeland.

"Faith is strong on both sides of the wall when believers meet to fellowship," the Dean told us. I knew how it felt to be separated from my family, but nothing stopped me when I wanted to return to them for a visit. Once again, my trials were trivial against the backdrop of the Separation Wall and the struggles of those who were divided by it. I would have been happy to end my journey right there and serve at the College, but that was not in the plan for me. We must always heed the voice of the Holy Spirit regardless of how we feel.

Meekness and Majesty

Our travels around Judea took us through the wilderness where Jesus had faced forty days of testing. The barren desert dunes and the oppressive heat confronted me with the reality of our human frailty and the severity of the temptations Jesus endured on our behalf. It left me very humbled and grateful for the Lord's obedience.

In stark contrast to the meekness and suffering of our Lord in the desert, the ruins of Masada, where Herod built one of his many majestic fortresses, reveals the extreme self-indulgence of a hedonistic maniac. This massive rock, standing 100 meters above the desert with a 450 meter drop to the Dead Sea, provided Herod with an unconquerable fortress. It was later used as a place of refuge for the Jewish Zionists fleeing the Romans. The Romans tried to annihilate the Jews, like so many others in history, but the Roman Empire fell. Masada still stands as a testimony and so does the Jewish nation.

Blessed be the name of God forever and ever, for wisdom and might are His. And He changes the times and the seasons; He removes kings and raises up kings; He gives wisdom to the wise and knowledge to those who have understanding.
— Daniel 2:20-21

Little Friends of the Desert

The Dead Sea lies 400 meters below sea level, the lowest land area on earth and fascinating enough to visit with a concentration of minerals and salts eight times saltier than the ocean. I wasn't feeling adventurous and it didn't look inviting enough for a swim; however, my team wasn't having me opt out.

"You cannot come all this way and not get in!" I was duly reprimanded and obediently went off to change my clothes. I wondered what lay underneath me as I floated on the salt-sea. Were the two cities (Sodom and Gomorrah) that failed to heed God's Word buried beneath?

We later ventured a little further into the desert to En Gedi, an oasis west of the Dead Sea where King David once hid from King Saul. Most in the group went on a hike up to the cave where David would have taken shelter and where he once cut off a piece of Saul's garments while he slept; others in the group rested around the oasis pool. I had another quest—this time I wanted to see things in the present not the past.

The small desert ibex frequent these parts and I guessed that they wouldn't be far from water. Finding a quiet spot behind a tree on the bank of the ravine, with camera ready in hand, I waited—my patience was shortly rewarded. A little mountain goat appeared directly below. It gracefully lifted its head to feed off an acacia branch while I quietly snapped away. Then patience was doubly rewarded—in a tree above me was a rock hyrax, another little friend of the desert.

The Stones Testify

Each place you stop at in Israel impacts you differently, but when on an intensely packed itinerary, one does not have time to process the experience before the next surprising encounter. I took many pictures and acquired many facts along the way from our knowledgeable leader that I was later able to research and assimilate.

Archaeology has supported the Biblical account of the fall of Jericho since the discovery of remnants of a collapsed city wall. The wall was uncovered in three parts, and on the north side, a house that was built into the wall is still standing. This could possibly have been Rahab's house, as from this side, it was only a short distance to the hills of Judea where the spies hid for three days (Joshua 2:16, 22).[45]

Jesus said that if we did not acknowledge Him, the stones would cry out.[46] The evidence of the stones testifying to Scripture is now overwhelming.

Jesus in My Boat

Our last stopover was at Ginnosar Kibbutz, and I was eager to see the 2,000-year-old fishing boat discovered in 1986 and carbon dated back to 40 B.C. It took a seven-year chemical preservation process before it could be put on display at the Kibbutz museum. This rudimentary sailing vessel is exactly the type of fishing boat that Jesus would have sailed in on the Sea of Galilee.

"Storms can stir up very quickly over the sea," Paul explained to us as we later boarded the "King David," a much larger replica. "And it poses a real threat to small boats." It was a perfectly calm day, but how would a small boat survive a calamitous one. I was intrigued and made of point of researching the weather of the area on my return. And true enough, the whole region is climatically complex. Conditions in the surrounding hills are extremely cool and dry, and when strong cold winds funnel through the hills descending on the warm, moist shallow sea, they can quickly whip up rogue waves.

I tried to imagine how the disciples might have felt in a small wooden boat when a squall hit. We know that even with Jesus in the boat, the disciples were still afraid.[47] It wasn't difficult to see the illustration of that experience as a pattern in my own life. When storms hit, instead of running straight to Jesus, who is always in my boat, I would examine the storm and thereby allow fear to infiltrate. Thankful for the lessons on the journey and the victory of the Cross, I have been able to overcome this.

The Mount of Beatitudes

We crossed the sea and stopped awhile on the Mount of Beatitudes while Paul ministered to us from the Scriptures. The Beatitudes (supreme blessedness) were taught by Jesus on this tranquil hill that overlooks the vast Lake of Galilee. It made me wonder why we have to sit in stuffy classrooms and lecture halls to gain an education when learning is best acquired amongst nature, and what better place than the sides and slopes of a mountain?

The eight blessings from Matthew chapter five are to the poor, the mournful, the meek, the hungry, the merciful, the pure in heart, the peacemakers, and the persecuted. I was wondering why the mirthful were not mentioned, after all Jesus came to give us abundant life with peace and joy, then, I looked across the lake towards Tiberius, a Roman settlement founded in 18 A.D. by Herod Antipas. This was one town that Jesus never visited. A stark reminder of the enemy's presence in their midst.

Inhabitable Hazor

On our last day we toured the northern regions of Galilee and visited the largest ancient Biblical site in Israel, the city of Hazor. Located on the trade route that connected the North with the Middle East and Egypt, and captured by Joshua on his Canaanite conquest, this ancient city continued to be a place of controversy throughout the times of the Old Testament, referred to as *"The head of all those kingdoms"* (Joshua 11:10b).

21 From Bethlehem to Megiddo

Jeremiah prophesied its demise:

Hazor shall be a dwelling for jackals, a desolation forever; no one shall reside there, nor son of man dwell in it.
— Jeremiah 49:33

Hazor now stands as Jeremiah had said it would, "a place of desolation forever"; one could sense the emptiness in the atmosphere.

Abraham's Gate

In ancient times the only place one could enter Canaan from the north was through a three arched gate, dating back to 18th century B.C. Perhaps the oldest gate still standing, the gate that Abraham would have entered through.[48] The three arches, for me, were significant of the Trinity, as Jesus said that *He* is the gate by which we must enter to have eternal life.[49]

Megiddo—the Final Battle

Then up on towards Mount Herman and the Golan Heights. Our final visit was Megiddo, a place of war and conflict for over a thousand years before Christ, and the site of the impending final battle.[50] Standing on the edge of the ruins of the fortress of Megiddo, I had a realistic view of the vastness of the valley of Jezreel that stretches out across 520 square kilometres.

Jesus' life on earth started in Bethlehem (House of Bread); He came first for the House of Israel (God contends).[51] The last battle to take place on earth is prophesied to be at Megiddo (Gathering for Cutting) and the valley of Jezreel (Sown of God). This battle is destined to be against the House of Israel because judgment for the whole world begins with Israel.[52] This enormous plain of Megiddo has staged many ancient battles, but the final battle will out-stage them all.

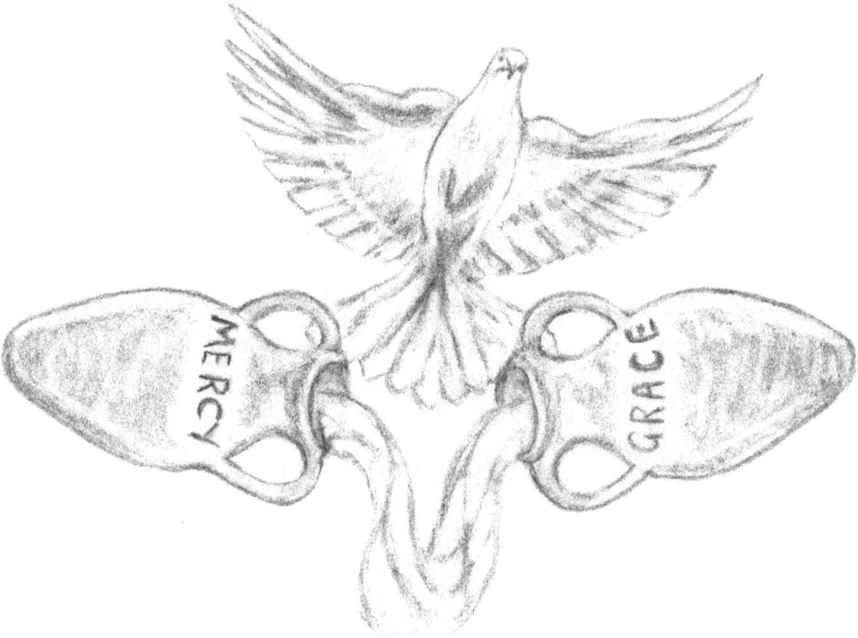

22
The Welsh Outpouring

After two days He will revive us; on the third day He will raise us up.
Hosea 6:2

𝓘T WAS A GUSTY APRIL Monday when I touched down at London's Heathrow airport; inspired and bursting to share my newly acquired knowledge, but once again, there was no time to take stock. That same week the little Welsh town of Cwmbran had experienced an outpouring of the Holy Spirit. It started with a man who had been wheelchair-bound for ten years. During a time of prayer, he was touched by God so powerfully that he jumped up out of his chair, picked it up over his head, and ran around the meeting place. The news soon carried out to all of England, Scotland, and beyond.

The local church in Sutton was abuzz with talk of the outpouring. Members of the fellowship who had relatives in Wales who witnessed the miracle healing were keeping us posted on the daily events. I listened to the reports and prayed for an opportunity to witness the outpouring myself. The meetings were continuing, six nights every week, and by the end of June, my door of opportunity opened. The intercessors were planning a trip to Wales, and I was invited to join them. We booked our seats on a coach and left for Wales one Friday afternoon. The traffic was heavy, as it always is when leaving London. I felt the throes of a migraine just two hours into our journey.

It was Saturday night when we finally arrived at the revival site. Queues of eager worshipers lined up outside an old warehouse. There was a large sign across the entrance that read: "Victory Church." I smiled to myself; it's not an elaborate building that Jesus is attracted to when He decides to pay a fellowship a visit. My migraine had reached a steady torturous throb and I seriously doubted that I would be able to sit through the service, but to my surprise, as I stepped into the building, I picked up on the atmosphere of joy and peace, and the throbbing subsided. When I entered the main hall, the migraine instantly ceased.

One cannot be nonchalant about the presence of God. We are emotional beings and the excitement was tangible. Sitting two rows from the drums, which under normal circumstances would not have been endurable, even without a headache, the volume had no negative impact. I was caught up in the worship instead. A dear lady behind me leaned over and said:

"Every service is different, expect the unexpected."

Believers from the USA and Australia testified to having flown over just to experience the outpouring. I believe that one cannot do justice in describing a visitation from the Lord—it needs to be encountered.

People too easily criticize what they don't understand or have never experienced. It's like the two Greek words for knowledge used in the New Testament: *Gnosis* and *Epignosis*. *Gnosis* is translated as intellectual knowledge while *epignosis* means upon knowledge or experiential knowledge. Revivals are *epignosis*, so I'm not going to diminish it in an effort to explain it, but a twelve-year old boy sitting next to me turned to me and said, *"This is the best day of my life!"*

The lady, in whose home I stayed for the rest of the weekend, ran a Bible study that the healed man attended. She told me how the muscles in his legs had atrophied over the years and how heavy the wheelchair was as she frequently lifted it into the boot of the car. And yet, the miracle was so complete that the man was able to instantly lift the chair and run with it.

*****

Wales is known as the "Land of Great Awakenings," starting in the 18th century with Howell Harris (1735) and then David Morgan (1859). The most well-known outpouring of the Spirit was in 1904/1905 lead by Evan Roberts, which resulted in over 150,000 converts.

Jesus Christ is the same yesterday, today, and forever (Hebrews 13:8). — **God can do it again!**

Mt. Taranaki

23
Land of the Long White Cloud

The great day of the Lord is near; it is near and hastens quickly.

Zephaniah 1:14a

*M*Y RESIDENT PERMIT FOR NEW Zealand finally arrived. I was able to spend my last month at Lincoln University teaching English to Chinese students. It was great to be with my Asian friends and talk about China again, but after my stint in Lincoln, I was happy to board a plane for Australia. Years of travel and adventure had taken its toll—I needed to anchor down and unwind. After a brief stopover with family in Sydney, I crossed the Tasman Sea for the island the early Polynesian settlers called Aotearoa, "Land of the Long White Cloud."

I unpacked my case, sent my walking shoes of seven years off to the tip, tucked away my new Swiss passport, and settled down to a time of rest in "Kiwi Land." I soon found myself combing for shells on one of Auckland's peaceful beaches and recalled the day, many years ago, when I once walked along a beach on the East Coast of Northern Natal and heard God telling me I would one day live in New Zealand. God is faithful and He makes all things beautiful in His time.

It was then that a revelation came to me from Hosea 2:14-15, the Scripture the Lord had given me at the start of my journey on leaving South Africa (Chapter 1). It spoke to me of the Church, from her birth and struggles throughout history to the preparation for the return of her bridegroom. We've been saying for years that the time of the Lord is near, and it is—one day in heaven is like a thousand years on earth. [53]

The following chapter is an interpretation of Hosea 2:14-15 as it alludes, for me, to the history of the Church.

24
A Door of Hope

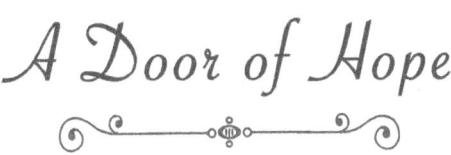

Therefore, behold, I will allure her, will bring her into the wilderness, and speak comfort to her. I will give her her vineyards from there, and the Valley of Achor as a door of hope; she shall sing there, as in the days of her youth, as in the day when she came up from the land of Egypt.

Hosea 2:14-15

I will allure her, I will bring her into the wilderness

BY THE TIME JERUSALEM WAS destroyed in 70 A.D., all the New Testament writings had been completed. And, by the end of the second century, all twenty-seven books of the New Testament had become the standard teachings of the early Church. The influence of Rome; however, soon began to infiltrate the infant Church. By A.D. 312, the edict of Toleration, issued by Constantine, had transformed the Church into the image of Rome. The edict granted freedom of religion for all, and *all* freely united their polytheistic deities and pagan practices with the Christian Church. The Scriptures became the property of the religious leaders of Rome and without the bread of life the Church was thrust into a spiritual desert with the Dark Ages following.

> "Behold, the days are coming," says the Lord God, "That I will send a famine on the land, not a famine of bread, nor a thirst for water, but of hearing the words of the Lord." — Amos 8:11

And speak comfort to her

Throughout the Dark Ages, between the 6th and 13th centuries, the medieval monks served as beacons of hope and comfort. The monks were the missionaries of that era. They took care of the orphans, the sick and dying, and offered shelter to travellers. They taught holiness and reverence towards God and they preserved the Scriptures by producing thousands of hand written copies of the Bible.

> I will bring the blind by a way they did not know; I will lead them in paths they have not known. I will make darkness light before them, And crooked places straight. These things I will do for them, And not forsake them.
> — Isaiah 42:16

I will give her her vineyards from there

The renaissance and reformation ushered in a new age of knowledge and spiritual awakening. With the invention of the printing press in 1456, the people were able to read their own printed Bible, and the land was refreshed with the "Bread of Life." The Reformation taught salvation through faith towards God apart from works. Through the study of the Scriptures,

24 A Door of Hope

the fruit of the Spirit was restored with peace and assurance of salvation.

> *You shall no longer be termed Forsaken ... for the Lord delights in you.* — Isaiah 62:4

And the Valley of Achor, a door of hope

The Holiness movement of the 18th and 19th centuries restored sanctification to the church. Hearts were renewed with joy in the many hymns of Charles Wesley. The Pentecostal Movement at the turn of the 20th century birthed revivals with manifestations of the gifts of the Spirit—a door of hope opened for the preparation for the Second Coming.

> *This will be written for the generation to come, that a people yet to be created may praise the* L<small>ORD</small>. — Psalm 102:18

She will sing there, as in the days of her youth, as in the day when she came up from the land of Egypt

The Charismatic renewal of the 1960's brought an outpouring of praise and worship, and the five-fold ministry for the equipping of the saints came to the forefront. The five-fold ministers are God's leaders for maturing His Bride.

> *Till we all come to the unity of the faith and of the knowledge of the Son of God, to a perfect man, to the measure of the stature of the fullness of Christ.* [54]

From out of Egypt He called His Son, (Hosea 11:1) and from out of the world He calls His Bride (2 Corinthians 6:17).

The Ministry of the Fir Tree

I continue to see the vision of the girl with bright amber hair standing amidst tall fir trees, and now, each time I see her, she gets a little older. She represents to me, the church growing into maturity.

The fir tree in the Hebrew transliteration is "berôsh." It is used for all conifers: the cypress, fir, juniper, and pine, and it symbolizes many good things:

- A symbol of majesty, used for building the Temple of Solomon (I Kings 5:5-6).
- A symbol of glory: "The fir tree shall glorify the sanctuary" (Isaiah 60:13).
- A symbol of joy, used for musical instruments (II Samuel 6:5).
- A symbol of hope: "The fir tree shall replace thorns" (Isaiah 55:13).
- A symbol of unbroken communion with God. The Prophet Hosea calls God's people to be like the fir tree that bares fruit for the Lord (Hosea 14:8).
- A symbol of safety, a place of safety for the stork to nest (Psalm 104: 16-17). The stork is symbol of discernment: "Even the stork knows her appointed times... but My people do not know the judgment of the Lord" (Jeremiah 8:7).

The fir tree ministers to us to grow in the glory of the Lord, to continue in hope and communion with the Lord, and to hold on to our peace and joy while we discern the times and wait for the judgment of the Lord.

25
Into All the World

And He said unto them, "Go into all the world and preach the gospel to every creature."

Mark 16:15

CALCULATING ACCORDING TO APOSTLE PETER'S statement, "With the Lord one day is as a thousand years, and a thousand years as one day," [55] my waiting 30 years to fulfill my dream of missions in China, and my visit to Israel, would be around 43 minutes to the Lord. God's timing is perfect in all He calls us to do.

Maybe your world is your home, or your place of work, or your community. Your mission starts wherever you are. We are not to wait until we feel ready. When the Lord calls, He equips, and we are made ready as we go.[56]

The work of the Lord is not meant to be a sensational work that impresses the world. We are destined to inherit the Kingdom of Heaven and the world is destined to pass away.[57] While Jesus was enduring heat and hunger for all of mankind in the Jordan Desert, King Herod was reclining in one of his 10-star fortresses being waited on hand and foot. Jesus was raised to the right hand of the Father in heaven, while King Herod was eaten by worms. [58]

We do not therefore, need mighty exploits and outstanding giftings to please God. The success of our work is not going to be determined by fame or fortune, but by fire.

> *Each one's work will become clear; for the Day will declare it, because it will be revealed by fire: and the fire will test each one's work, of what sort it is.* — 1 Corinthians 3:13

Worship in the Waiting

Serving the Lord is a walk of obedience. After waiting until he was 100 years old, Abraham was given the promised son and then later told to sacrifice him. He wasn't given an explanation, nor did he demand one, he just did what he was told to do. He had no audience to applaud him for his brave act of obedience. God was his audience and his provider, sparing Isaac's life for a substitute ram. [59]

Thankfully, Jesus was our final sacrifice; He was offered once to bear the sins of many. [60] We now are called to offer our lives in service.

> *I beseech you therefore, brethren, by the mercies of God, that you present your bodies as a living sacrifice, holy, acceptable to God, which is your reasonable service.* — Romans 12:1

We, too, endure periods of waiting when all doors are closed, and often when a door finally opens, it may lead to more testing. In times when there appears to be little progress, the Lord is still working in us according to His good pleasure. [61] He is growing and equipping us for the next step.

> *For the vision is yet for an appointed time; but at the end it will speak, and it will not lie. Though it tarries, wait for it; because it will surely come, it will not tarry.* — Habakkuk 2:3

25   Into All the World

God sees the bigger picture; the whole plan for His church, whereas we see only the small part where we are involved. When the reality of the present brings doubt and unbelief, He gives us vision for the future. Waiting is often the most difficult part. Worship the Lord in the waiting.

For since the beginning of the world men have not heard nor perceived by the ear, nor has the eye seen any God besides You, who acts for the one who waits for Him.   — Isaiah 64:4

When He is ready to bring change into our lives, it comes swiftly and it is accompanied with an inner peace. Everything in the change is good, and always for the greater good of the whole Kingdom. We do not know what great impact our small acts of obedience have in the spiritual realm and what great achievements they serve for the Kingdom of God, whether we think they're of value or not.

Spiritual Awakenings

The spiritual awakenings that started in 1886 with the mission work of Pastor Pierson, of Philadelphia, spearheaded a great movement of foreign missions that accelerated into the twentieth century. He recorded the following in his writings on *The Crisis of Missions:*

The grace of God appears in missions, especially in working mighty results and effects, such as are plainly attributable only to the Divine Spirit. These results are wrought not only in individuals, but sometimes in whole communities; there are some transformations that deserve to be called transfigurations. [62]

Times of refreshing and outpourings have continued all over the world ever since. However, they will never be announced on world news, or in the local newspapers—that's where you find the world's events, not God's. In recent years, Africa has been visited with spiritual outpourings in Uganda. And in the North, from Mauritania to Libya, thousands of Muslims have come to know Christ as their Saviour and thousands more are streaming into Europe where they can be freely evangelized. The underground church in China is growing rapidly and so is the body of Christ in the Ukraine. Revivals and outpourings awaken the church to maturity, to put away the things of the world for the virtues of the Kingdom of God. [63]

> *Come, and let us return to the Lord; for He has torn, but He will heal us; He has stricken, but He will bind us up. After two days He will revive us; on the Third day He will raise us up, that we may live in His sight.* — Hosea 6:1-2

Appointed Times

The Lord is calling us to be sensitive to His appointed times. When judgment comes upon the ungodly, the only safe place is Jesus. Jesus is returning for a bride without spot or blemish, set apart from the things of the world [64] and in continual communion with Him. [65]

> *All the days of my hard service I will wait, till my change comes.* — Job 14:14

The Lord will perfect that which concerns you.[66] Let us not grow weary while doing good, for in due season we shall reap if we do not lose heart. [67] Rather, let us wait patiently until the right door opens, and then walk carefully in fellowship with Him into all the world.

25 Into All the World

From Season to Season He Changes us

Sharon was the first to return to the US to assist in a family crisis. She lives in Kansas where she progresses in her teaching career and ministers through music in the worship team of her local church. Although China is her first love, she obediently remains in the US as she feels the Lord instructing her to, witnessing to Chinese and other international students whenever the opportunity arises.

Bryan, after leaving China, travelled to the Middle East to teach English for three years. His teaching career now continues in Houston, Texas where he has since become happily married.

Kate moved on to a graduate school in Denmark where she studied Chinese and International Relations. She then returned to China where she currently works on a management and research program for an American land policy think tank.

Simon completed a post-graduate degree in accounting in the USA. He has settled in New York where he works for a firm of accountants. He is still trusting in God's divine favour.

Peter (not his real name) continues to serve in China, holding English Corners and sharing the Gospel to the Chinese. His ministry currently extends to facilitating Bible translation with MAST (Mobilized Assistance Supporting Translation) where he has worked on several Indian and African languages. His work also includes the International Orality Network for the Oral learners.

Belinda returned to South Africa for a short visit after completing her Masters in the UK. While driving to a church prayer meeting, she heard God telling her to remain in SA. This meant sacrificing her career dreams in continuing her sports medical research. She chose to be obedient and spent the following year at home, unemployed. During that time she grew in intimacy with God which remains, as she says: *"One of the most special times in my life."*

She now works for a pharmaceutical company and although her current position is not the job of her dreams, she has met, by God's grace, the man of her dreams. She remains faithful to the call that obedience to God and the people she is sent to serve is more important than career. She says, *"Every season in life has shaped me and drawn me closer to Jesus, teaching me more of His character and goodness."*

The author is happily settled in New Zealand, serving on the board of a Mission Language School in South Auckland, and coaching and counselling when needed. *'Apples of Gold, Adventures in the Underworld,* with some of Belinda's illustrations is now available on amazon.com.

From season to season He changes us and works in us according to His good pleasure.

25 Into All the World

If you have never received Jesus as your Personal Lord and Saviour, or if you are unsure of your salvation, then I invite you to pray this prayer in faith, believing that:

God so loved the world that He gave His only begotten Son, that whoever believes in Him should not perish, but have everlasting life. — John 3:16

For with the heart one believes unto righteousness, and with the mouth confession is made unto salvation. — Romans 10:10

JESUS SAID: "If anyone serves Me, let him follow Me; and where I am, there My servant will be also. If anyone serves Me, him My Father will honour." — John 12: 26

Prayer:

"Father God, I confess that I am a sinner in need of salvation.

I repent of my sins and acknowledge that Jesus Christ alone paid the price for my salvation. He alone has the authority to forgive sins (1 John 1:9, Matthew 9:6). I receive Jesus as my personal saviour, and I confess that Jesus Christ is Lord."

Reference Notes

Foreword

[1] Mark 12:30
[2] Mark 16:15
[3] Acts 1:8

Chapter 1

[4] Psalms 37:3
[5] 1 Peter 5:8
[6] Revelation 3:8

Chapter 4

[7] 1 Chronicles 4:18
[8] W. Whiston, Hendrickson, *Antiquities of the Jews,* Publishers, USA, Jan. 1995, Book 2, chapter 9:5-7
[9] Matthew 1:5
[10] Matthew 1:5
[11] Matthew 15:24
[12] John 4:28-43
[13] Matthew 5:30
[14] Acts 2:9

Chapter 6

[15] Daniel 11
[16] Carl G. Rasmussen, *Zondervan NIV Atlas Of The Bible,* Zondervan, Grand Rapids, Michigan, 1999, pp. 71, 130.
[17] Jeremiah 18:6
[18] Galatians 1:18-21
[19] Massouri, Department of Natural Resources, Massouri Limestone, Massouri Geological Survey. Accessed January, 2016. http://dnr.mo.gov/geology/geosrv/imac/limestone.htm

Chapter 7

[20] Ancient Civilizations http://www.ushistory.org/civ/9b.asp

[21] Kang, C.H. *The Discovery of Genesis*, p. 59

[22] Ibid, p. 57

[23] Ibid, p. 68

[24] Ibid p. 95

[25] Isaiah 49:11-12

[26] Thong, C.K. *Finding God in Ancient China,* chapter 4, pp.111-151 ___.

[27] Ibid, pp. 113, 116

[28] Most of the Great Wall visible today was rebuilt by the Ming Dynasty - 1368–1644 A.D.

[29] "Li" is a traditional word used to measure distance - about 500 meters in modern terms

[30] Wang Shanshan Stones indicate earlier Christian link? 2005-12-22, China Daily. Accessed January, 2016. http://www.chinadaily.com.cn/english/doc/2005-12/22/content_505587.htm

[31] Daleinchina, *The Jesus Petroplyph,* April 10, 2011, Daleinchina's Blog. Accessed January, 2016. https://daleinchina.wordpress.com/2011/04/10/the-jesus-petroglyph/

[32] 1 Kings 19:18

Chapter 9

[33] 1 John 4:18

Chapter 14

[34] J.R. Church, *Hidden Prophecies of the Psalms,* pp. 267 – 270.

[35] Nissan 1 was Passover, a time when shepherds were out in the fields watching over the lambs that were to be sold for sacrifice at the Temple.

Chapter 18

[36] Proverbs 29:18
[37] Proverbs 11:14b

Chapter 20

[38] John 19:41-42
[39] Matthew 27:59-60
[40] Isaiah 53:9
[41] Matthew 27:57; Mark 15:43
[42] Luke 22:42
[43] Tel Aviv University, "*Devastating Earthquake May Threaten Middle East's Near Future, Geologist Predicts*," Science Daily News, Oct. 4, 2007. sciencedaily.com. Accessed Jan, 2016. http://www.sciencedaily.com/releases/2007/10/071003142432.htm

Chapter 21

[44] Psalm 122:6
[45] Bryant G. Wood, PhD. "*The Walls of Jericho*," Jun. 9, 2009, Associates for Biblical Research. Accessed Jan. 2016, biblearchaeology.org. http://www.biblearchaeology.org/post/2008/06/The-Walls-of-Jericho.aspx#Article
[46] Luke 19:40
[47] Matthew 8:24-25
[48] Genesis 12:4-6; 14:14
[49] John 10:7-9
[50] Revelation 16:16
[51] Matthew 15:24; Romans 2:10
[52] Romans 2:9

Reference Notes

Chapter 23

[53] 2 Peter 3:8

Chapter 24

[54] Ephesians 4:11-13

Chapter 25

[55] 2 Peter 3:8
[56] Hebrews 13:21
[57] 1 John 2:15-17
[58] Acts 12:23
[59] Genesis 22:8-13
[60] Hebrews 9:28
[61] Philippians 2:12-13
[62] Pierson, A.T., *The Crisis of Missions*, page 13, Carter & Brothers, NY, 1886.
[63] 1 John 2:15
[64] Ephesians 5:27
[65] Romans 12:1
[66] Psalms 138:8
[67] Galatians 6:9

Thank you for reading *When All Doors Close*. If it has blessed you in any way, I would appreciate your taking a moment to write a review on Amazon, as well as on other sites like Barnes and Noble, Christian Book and in social media. This will greatly help me in getting the exposure this book needs. For example, at this writing, Amazon has it set up that if I get 50 reviews there, then when a customer buys a similar book, Amazon will say, "Customers who bought this item also bought..." and will include *When All Doors Close* in the list.

If you send the links to your reviews (just copy and paste the addresses from the browser) to my publisher (olivepressbooks@gmail.com), we would like to thank you with a free gift.

I am grateful to have you join me in encouraging others to do God's exciting and adventurous Kingdom work and that when it seems like a door has closed, they only need to wait to see God's plan unfold.

– Desiree Pfister

When All Doors Close

is available at:

olivepresspublisher.com

amazon.com

barnesandnoble.com

christianbook.com

deepershopping.com

and other online stores

Store managers:

Order wholesale through:

Ingram Book Company or

Spring Arbor

or by emailing:

olivepressbooks@gmail.com

www.ingramcontent.com/pod-product-compliance
Lightning Source LLC
Chambersburg PA
CBHW070657100426
42735CB00039B/2176